"I loved this book. It's practical, insightful, and most importantly, motivating to draw closer to our spouses. Rick is a wonderful writer who inspires."

—**Jim Burns, PhD**, president, HomeWord;
author of *Creating an Intimate Marriage*, *Closer*,
and *Getting Ready for Marriage*

"Rick Johnson's work is always a gift! A humorous, insightful, practical gift to the reader. *Romancing Your Better Half* is full of not just wise advice but ultra-practical steps for how to ensure your marriage continues to be something that you will enjoy and treasure for a lifetime. Which means Rick's latest book is something couples will treasure too!"

—**Shaunti Feldhahn**, social researcher and bestselling
author of *For Women Only*, *For Men Only*,
and *The Surprising Secrets of Highly Happy Marriages*

"Rick Johnson encourages men to be men and women to be women. That's refreshing. Written in his candid and engaging style, *Romancing Your Better Half* is going to reignite and, very likely, rescue thousands of marriages. Not by ripping down and rebuilding. Instead, Rick invites husbands and wives to look at marriage from each other's viewpoint. It's brilliant! Suddenly the secrets to romance and intimacy aren't secret anymore."

—**Jay Payleitner**, producer, speaker, and bestselling author
of *52 Things Husbands Need from Their Wives*

Romancing Your Better Half

Keeping INTIMACY *Alive* in YOUR MARRIAGE

Rick Johnson

Revell

a division of Baker Publishing Group
Grand Rapids, Michigan

© 2015 by Rick Johnson

Published by Revell
a division of Baker Publishing Group
P. O. Box 6287, Grand Rapids, MI 49516-6287
www. revellbooks. com

Printed in the United States of America

Library of Congress Cataloging-in-Publication Data
Johnson, Rick, 1956-
    Romancing your better half : keeping intimacy alive in your marriage / Rick Johnson.
        pages cm
    Includes bibliographical references.
    ISBN 978-0-8007-2234-0 (pbk.)
    1. Marriage—Religious aspects—Christianity. 2. Intimacy (Psychology)—Religious aspects—Christianity. I. Title.
    BV835.J645 2015
    248.8′44—dc23   2014030731

Author is represented by WordServe Literary Group.

15 16 17 18 19 20 21   7 6 5 4 3 2 1

In keeping with biblical principles of creation stewardship, Baker Publishing Group advocates the responsible use of our natural resources. As a member of the Green Press Initiative, our company uses recycled paper when possible. The text paper of this book is composed in part of post-consumer waste.

To the love of my life
and the best wife a man could ever hope for—

my Suzanne

There are several kinds of love. One is a selfish, mean, grasping, egotistical thing which uses love for self-importance. This is the ugly and crippling kind. The other is an outpouring of everything good in you—of kindness and consideration and respect—not only the social respect of manners but the greater respect which is recognition of another person as unique and valuable. The first kind can make you sick and small and weak but the second can release in you strength, and courage and goodness and even wisdom you didn't know you had.

—John Steinbeck

People always fall in love with the most perfect aspects of each other's personalities. Who wouldn't? Anybody can love the most wonderful parts of another person. But that's not the clever trick. The really clever trick is this: Can you accept the flaws? Can you look at your partner's faults honestly and say, "I can work around that. I can make something out of it"? Because the good stuff is always going to be there, and it's always going to be pretty and sparkly, but the crap underneath can ruin you.

—Elizabeth Gilbert,
*Committed: A Skeptic
Makes Peace with Marriage*

What if God didn't design marriage to be "easier"? What if God had an end in mind that went beyond our happiness, our comfort, and our desire to be infatuated and happy as if the world were a perfect place? *What if God designed marriage to make us holy more than to make us happy?*

—Gary Thomas,
Sacred Marriage

Contents

Acknowledgments

A book is an insentient entity that has life breathed into it by an innumerable amount of people during its creation. In some ways it parallels the story of Frankenstein's monster.

The author of a book actually has only a small part of its development. Here is my perception of the process involved, at least when I write books (probably most writers have their own unique experience):

The writer (me) has the initial idea, then the acquisitions editor begins the process by seeing that vision and submitting it to the publishing committee for approval. Once the acquisition of a book is approved, a contract is negotiated by an agent and all sorts of secretive (and likely tightfisted) accounting types at the publishing house, then an initial draft of the manuscript is written over many months. It is then reviewed by the acquisitions editor, who throws out most of the junk and molds and twists the material into something resembling an actual book. After rewrites and excruciating

9

revisions (all under an extremely short deadline), the inno-cent writer then resubmits it to the editor, who fine-tunes it and again snips and gouges out all the "garbage" (usually the best stuff) the writer tried to sneak back into the text. After that, the manuscript is submitted to an in-house line editor who parses each sentence and picks it to death. Every word is looked at and compared to every word ever written in the history of the world. After another round of revisions guaranteed to bring out the pettiness in my nature, the book is formatted into its printed format called galleys. The galleys are sent back to the author to review for the 5,000th time and any final changes are incorporated before going to print. All this is happening while the poor writer is trying to work on his current manuscript as well.

During this entire process the author is also working on the next manuscript; marketing a previous book through social media, radio, and television interviews; filling out marketing and titling scripts; writing blogs for blog tours; developing leadership study guides for the book; thinking up and con-tacting potential endorsers and people of influence to send the book to; creating a list of people who contributed to the book and get a free copy and a list of people who want a free book to write a review; recording radio spots; approv-ing cover artwork; and generally about 400 other things at the same time.

All that whining and complaining aside, I seem to be one of the few lucky individuals who has made a full-time living as a writer for the past nine years. That's not because I'm such a great writer, but more because I have such a great team of people supporting me and making my books better as well as getting them into the hands of my faithful readers. These people are the real heroes behind the scene as they put up with all my snarling and griping and still seem to like working with me (or else they are just very professional and have me fooled). They probably do twice the work under much more stressful conditions than I do, because each of them is working with a plethora of authors all at the same time.

Here's an abbreviated list (not in order of importance) of people on my team without whom I would be a miserable flop: Dr. Vicki Crumpton, Michele Misiak, Claudia Marsh, Greg Johnson, Cheryl Van Andel, Barb Barnes, Mary Molegraaf, Erin Bartels, Pat VanderWeide, Robin Barnett, Twila Bennett, the design staff, warehouse staff, and the sales team at Revell, as well as probably another couple dozen people that I don't even know about who have their fingerprints on this book. Thank you!

Introduction

Being married is one of the greatest gifts we can give ourselves. A large body of research confirms that married couples are happier, they live longer, they are healthier, they are better off financially, and they have fewer psychological problems than people who are not married. Americans also highly value marriage—when surveyed, people consistently rate a good marriage and having a happy, healthy family as their most important goals.

So if marriage is so good for people and society, why can about half of current marriages expect to end in divorce? Why are young people increasingly reluctant to marry—they yearn for a lifelong loving relationship but are skeptical of its possibility? Why are about 40 percent of children born out of wedlock and likely will not have a marriage relationship modeled for them? These children are significantly more inclined than kids born and raised in a "traditional" family to have children out of wedlock themselves. Are we seeing the results of the disintegration of marriage in our culture today? If so, how do we erase the decline and help people understand the value of a good marriage?

Just like laying a stable and solid foundation is the key to building a house that lasts, building a solid foundation for our relationship is one of the important keys for a marriage that lasts. The structure of that foundation is a relationship based on healthy intimacy, which in turn creates an environment where couples can grow together long enough for a deep and nurturing love to take place.

I'll admit right up front that I don't claim to be some kind of expert on what women want or need in a relationship (and I'd be pretty skeptical of anyone who did make that claim), or even a decent judge of what romance and intimacy in a marriage looks like. But I have managed to stay married to the same woman for thirty-two years as of this writing. That qualifies as a minor miracle nowadays (especially considering our personal family backgrounds) with the high rate of divorce and multiple marriages. Surprisingly, it's not because my wife has low expectations for intimacy and romance. She's a beautiful, intelligent woman who could have had her pick of a high percentage of the male population from around the world. But all that to say, I've picked up a few pointers and insights along the way about living with a woman and making her reasonably happy and satisfied. And since I *am* a man and have worked with thousands of other men, I have a pretty good idea of the things that a man needs most in a relationship.

Marriage hasn't been easy, but I will say that persevering through the tough times is a satisfaction in and of itself. The bonding that has occurred by going through the struggles, the good times, and the bizarre occurrences of life has created a comfortable and deeply peaceful intimate relationship as the years have progressed.

The truth is that love and marriage are difficult. When Hollywood and Madison Avenue sugarcoat them and make romance seem like a walk in the park, they do a great disservice in creating unrealistic expectations for millions of young couples.

Loving a woman is, on the one hand, very easy. On the other, it is very difficult—sometimes nearly impossible. Frequently it doesn't take much to make a woman happy—a kind word, an unexpected expression of love, or a romantic gesture with no expectations. Other times, no matter what a man does, it is never enough. Likewise, women probably find men perplexing as well (although nowhere near as complicated).

Most men, if they are lucky, marry "up." They value their wives as a greater "prize" than they deserve. My wife is a better wife than I am a husband. She's certainly a better person than I am, and if I'm being honest, she's likely a more mature Christian as well. Not only that, but she probably rates higher on most of the positive character traits than I do. She's more compassionate, tolerant, patient, loving, kind, gentle, caring, and humble than I am. She might even be more honest, faithful, loyal, and good than I am (okay, maybe more intelligent as well). I'm a lot stronger physically than she is, but that might be the only advantage I've got on her. (This works well for my main roles around the house as jar opener, garbage remover, bug killer, and heavy furniture mover.)

I've noticed that there are times in life when everything just seems to go right. I have experienced these phenomena in sports, in business, and in relationships. For brief periods of time nothing you do can go wrong. In sports they call it being in the "zone." Every basket you shoot goes in, every baseball coming toward the batter's box looks as big as a beach ball, and every pass you throw is perfect. You feel "at one" with the field or court, your teammates, and the flow of the game. In business there are usually short periods of time when every decision pays off. You feel like King Midas—everything you touch turns to gold.

And there are times in a relationship when things go perfectly—when you are in the zone. When she gets and actually appreciates all my jokes (instead of getting offended), when I am able to artfully articulate exactly how I feel, when I am smooth and suave in everything I do, and when she looks at me like I am all that matters in the world. That "zone" to my wife probably looks like this: he focuses all his attention on me without being distracted, he spends time with me, he's open and shares his innermost thoughts and feelings with me, he treats me like a queen.

Those times probably seem to be infrequent to both spouses, but they happen just often enough to encourage us to have hope. Hope that they will come again—usually when least expected. Those marriage "zones" are when my world seems best. Like the infrequent surprise sunny day in Oregon, they make all the other dreary times seem worthwhile.

My goal with this book is to give you as many tips (or keys or nuggets or whatever you want to call them) to help you slide into those zones as often and easily as possible. Because when you learn how to create and then appreciate those times in the zone, you create a lasting and fulfilling marriage. And your marriage matters—to you, your family, and our culture.

1

Marriage

Together Forever?

It's supposed to be hard. If it wasn't hard,
everyone would do it. The hard is what
makes it great.

—Coach Jimmy Dugan in
A League of Their Own

Most men were initially drawn to their wives like moths to a flame. Many of us were just stumbling along, minding our own business (happy in our bachelorhood) when *Pow!*—out of the blue we were dumbstruck by the power of this strange but beautiful and beguiling creature. We didn't know why we were attracted to her (although she certainly caught our attention with her looks), but we just knew we wanted to be close to her and spend time with her. We had an irresistible urge to smooch on her all the time. We longed to be around her when she was absent but were dumbstruck speechless when she was present. She made us feel thick and substantial while floaty and weightless at the same time. We were rendered dizzy by the aroma that followed her around like a flitting butterfly, tantalizingly alighting on the tips of our noses. Her voice was like a siren of Greek mythology causing us not to wreck ourselves upon rocks but to desire to share our most secret dreams with her that we never told anyone (which was maybe just as dangerous). Some of these dreams we never even knew ourselves. But we knew, we knew in our heart, that this was the woman who made us want to be a better man. To conquer the world and lay it at her feet like a puppy seeking his mistress's approval.

I knew on our second date that my wife-to-be was the "one." She gave me a postcard that simply said, "I believe in you." No one had ever told me that before. All I knew was, I wanted to be the man she put her faith in. I needed to be that man.

When a man and woman come together as one, their individual strengths and weaknesses complement each other, making them more powerful as a team than either of them are individually. Make no mistake, though, marriage is difficult. It may well be the hardest relationship we will ever experience in our lifetime. I've found that nothing *worthwhile* in life is ever easy. In fact, the things that matter most are often the most difficult—things like marriage, raising children, significant accomplishments, etc. That means that the marriage experience, if done properly, is one of the most satisfying and enjoyable experiences we can undertake—even with all of its struggles and hardships.

Perhaps there is a good reason that marriage is difficult. Oftentimes the experiences we have with other people that are the most challenging, stretching, and even wounding are those that bond us closest together. If that's true, then maybe marriage isn't meant to be easy. Because it's the most important relationship you'll ever enter into, you can expect to have some of the deepest struggles you'll ever encounter. Maybe the very fact that it *is* so difficult ensures that it is a worthwhile endeavor. I know, *Easy for you to say sitting behind the computer keyboard—you don't know my spouse*, but trust me, I've had my share of marital challenges over the past thirty-two years. The one thing you won't find in this book is an author who thinks he knows everything about marriage and has had a perfect relationship with his wife. I've made as many mistakes as anyone reading this book.

That said, those kinds of experiences are the very thing that help others learn from and hopefully keep from making the same mistakes. And it's worth it, because married people are healthier, happier, and better off financially than their single counterparts. Having a spouse means you have someone to rely on to help shoulder the burdens of life and raising a family. You are responsible for each other. You care about each other's well-being, mental health, and financial situation.[1]

Marriage allows each partner to develop certain skills while not having to be "perfect" at everything. We can count on our spouse to be responsible for the things he or she is good at, allowing us to focus on those things we excel in. Marriage also gives us a person to depend on and to face the stresses of life with together.

Perhaps because of those factors, research shows that married people are physically and emotionally healthier and live longer than their single counterparts. Married men and women both report less depression, anxiety, and lower levels of other types of psychological stress. Single people have much higher mortality rates (50 percent higher for women and 250 percent higher for men) than married people. Women tend to live longer when married because they have more money and live in better neighborhoods with adequate health care (statistics show that just over half of single women have health insurance, as opposed to 83 percent of married women). Married men tend to live longer because they stop risky behaviors such as drinking, drugs, driving fast (while intoxicated), and putting themselves in a variety of dangerous situations. Married men also have much better diets and their wives monitor their health and force them to see the doctor when necessary. [2]

Nearly all Americans (93 percent) rate "having a happy marriage" as either one of the most important or very important goals in life, even outpacing "good health" and "good family life." The number one goal of high school seniors is to "have a good marriage and family life." [3]

Despite the pressures today to change or even abolish traditional marriage, individuals and society clearly benefit from this institution.

What Is Marriage?

> [Marriage] is the merciless revealer, the great white searchlight turned on the darkest places of human nature.
>
> —Katherine Anne Porter

Two (usually young) people start out in life together under the bliss of hormone-induced euphoria. They have well-intentioned but unrealistic ideas of what their lives together will be like. What starts out as an innocent, uncorrupted, and pure bud of love over the years morphs into an old gnarled, scarred, and weather-beaten tree stump of friendship and devotion. And yet within this hoary old trunk beats a vibrant heart of the strongest white oak hardened by its perseverance and longevity to withstand any challenge that man, beast, or Mother Nature can throw against it. Those marriages that last for decades begin to discover the peaceful joy and contentedness that can only come from a lifetime of companionship and working together to rise above obstacles.

Many partners enter into marriage as frauds—showing only the best of themselves. But marriage has a tendency to expose the truth about two people and shine light on their true character. What was kept secretly under wraps while dating soon becomes apparent in the light of day during marriage.

When that happens, the character of the individuals either nourishes the relationship or destroys it. A healthy marriage relationship is comprised of the traits of trust, honesty, humor, faith, and commitment. Marriage in turn teaches us patience, selflessness, and humility.

Overcoming challenges is what makes us successful and grows us as human beings. Whether in a sporting event, at the workplace, or in a science lab, the person who is able to overcome the greatest difficulties is celebrated as a winner. Why should marriage be any different? When the hardships of a relationship confront us, we shouldn't easily quit but rather give it the same effort we would any other worthwhile challenge in life. Certainly a good marriage is more important than throwing a basketball through a hoop in the larger scheme of things, yet people go to great lengths to improve themselves in sports when they won't spend nearly as much energy trying to overcome minor obstacles in their marriage.

Perhaps the greatest compliment we can get from our spouse (especially after a decade or two of being married) is to hear that if they could do it all over, they would marry us again. To have that person—who knows our core character with all its ugly faults and basest venalities—actually *want* to go through the dark challenges, abject failures, and deep wounds of life all over together again means that they are either insane or that this kind of love is worth every obstacle we must face in order to achieve it.

Some common stressors in marriage consist of the lack of communication (or miscommunication), avoiding important issues, financial struggles, overscheduling of our time, addictions, and living in crisis. Bad relationships between unhealthy people tend to be smothered in chaos. When people live in chaos it's extremely difficult for the relationships or the individuals to grow beyond getting their immediate needs met. Those relationships spend all their time and energy just running around putting out fires.

Psychologist Abraham Maslow's Hierarchy of Needs posits that if you can't get your most basic needs met you can't focus on higher concepts like love and intimacy. It's difficult if not impossible to move from one level up to the next one until that need has been fulfilled. Once the foundational level of a person's needs are met—like their physical needs (food, water, shelter, etc.)—then a person can move into the next level of development, and so on, until they finally reach the top level of self-actualization. So, for instance, if a woman lives in an unsafe environment or struggles keeping the utilities turned on or from getting evicted from her home, she's not likely to be able to work on her self-esteem or growing intimacy in her personal relationships. The "depression of poverty" keeps people from having the desire or ability to move forward in life and make healthy choices.

Maslow's Hierarchy of Needs

The healthier we get, the further up Maslow's pyramid we progress and the greater the likelihood that we will be able to sustain healthy relationships with those in our lives. This is one reason why I am telling my young adult daughter that *now* (while she is *not* in a relationship) is the time to grow herself and heal any wounds—so that when the right young man comes along she will be in a position to take advantage of entering into a healthier marriage. Since we tend to marry a person who is at the same level of emotional maturity as we are, it only makes sense to be as healthy as possible in order to find the healthiest mate, thus giving ourselves a better chance of having a successful relationship.

What Does Marriage Take?

Success in marriage does not come merely through finding the right mate, but through being the right mate.

—Barnett R. Brickner

Marriage is as much a business partnership as it is a romance. Even though our culture heavily promotes the unrealistic concept that marriage is a fifty-fifty proposition, it's important to remember that it's more about mutual submission to one another's needs and desires than it is absolute equality. To have an "absolute equality" mentality creates ongoing disappointment and resentment. More important is that each partner feels like they are invested in the relationship and contributing. Sometimes it seems like one spouse is giving 95 percent while the other is only contributing 5 percent toward the marriage. In those circumstances it's important to trust that your spouse will carry more than their fair share at some later date. That requires being a servant-hearted spouse even when we don't feel like it. It also requires being proactive and intentional in your commitment to serve your spouse.

Right after each of our children were born, my wife had to devote all her energies to healing herself and nurturing these helpless newborn babies. Therefore I took over all the chores she normally did as well as my own duties. So for a period of time I did *all* the dishes, laundry, housecleaning, and other things necessary to run a household. But I knew that when appropriate, my wife would return to her normal duties and at some time in the future (like when I was ill) she would take over more than her share of the everyday chores for a short period of time. This is a sign of a healthy relationship.

It's virtually impossible to split every task equally down the middle. Besides, one partner might be much better (more capable, interested, or experienced) at some tasks than others, and allowing each spouse to do their share of chores that fit their skill set is a much more efficient and expedient process. What's important is that each partner believes they and their spouse are contributing something of value that benefits the relationship. When we do that, it allows us to produce more as a team than we could produce individually. Ultimately, marriage is more about giving than it is about getting.

A marriage requires nearly continual forgiveness (both requesting and granting) from both spouses in order to work. If you can't extend that kind of grace, you can't expect to receive it either. It necessitates the willingness to compromise—by both partners. Without the ability to forgive, the wounded person soon becomes the wounder. In addition, forgiveness (along with gratitude) appears to be the number one trait linked to happiness in marriage—and possibly in life. When you are able to forgive each other, you don't carry around all that resentment and anger bottled up inside. This is important because all those resentments (even from outside sources) eventually get taken out on one person—our spouse. If we can't learn to regularly forgive and forget, we become bitter, frustrated critics—unable to see the beauty in life or the blessing of our spouse.

Even strong Christian marriages face the same challenges as any other marriage: communication problems, sexual temptations, frustrations, and unrealized expectations. Without the ability to forgive each other, those pressures erode the foundation of your marriage and create disappointment and resentment.

Having a good marriage also requires us to prioritize our marriage. We have to be willing to make time for one another and take steps to improve our marriage. Activities like reading books, attending workshops and conferences, being part of a small study group, and seeking counseling if necessary are vital to ensure a growing and healthy marriage relationship. If we allow busyness, weariness, an unhealthy past, or a lack of replenishing relationships in our life to interfere with our timetable, we are unable to prioritize our spouse and give them the attention they deserve. Most of us work at least eight hours a day. Throw in travel time, shopping, and sleep and you've taken up most of the rest of the day. Oh yes, then throw a handful of kids into the mix along with their sports, music, camps, and other activities and . . . wow! I'm tired just writing about it. It's no wonder I hear all the time comments from parents like, "I'm exhausted" or "I'm so busy I don't have time for myself" or "We haven't even had sex in a month" or finally "Our marriage revolves around the kids. I'm not sure we even love each other anymore."

It's human nature to spend our most precious commodity— our time—on the things we value most. So when I hear men say they love their kids more than their job, but they spend twelve hours a day working and miss all their kids' games and recitals, I have to question whether their actions back up their words or not. Or when a woman says she values her marriage but spends all of her energy investing in her children with no time for her husband, I question where her values really are. It's important for parents to remember that your marriage will still be around long after your kids are gone. And it's worth staying together for the long run. Even though our kids are grown and gone (most of the time), I'd be lost without my wife. She knows me better than anyone in the entire world. She cares about me more than anyone else in the world. She appreciates my ugly old self better than anyone else could. To think of ending that and having to expend the energy to try to build that all over with someone else is daunting to even consider. But building that kind of relationship takes time. It isn't done overnight or even over years. It takes decades.

Being grateful is a big part of a successful marriage. Appreciating your spouse and the sacrifices they make is part of being happy and contented with our life and marriage. We all just want to be appreciated. It's amazing what a simple "thank you" will do for your relationship.

Lastly, to have a long-term successful marriage also requires having the devotion to place another's wants and needs ahead of your own—not a natural trait (at least for most men). It requires the discipline to deny ourselves the pleasures and desires that we selfishly and sometimes desperately crave, with no guarantee that we will be "rewarded" or will benefit from that self-sacrifice. A good marriage depends upon this trust as the stabilizing force that keeps each partner from desecrating the vows made when their love was strong and unassailable. I know that after all our years together, Suzanne will still always place my well-being in the forefront of every decision she makes. She would never intentionally seek to harm me or betray me in any way. And I believe she feels I will do the same for her. This confidence, though, has been built (tested and proven) over a long time of devotion on both our parts.

Why Your Marriage Matters

> Divorce, by definition, is a failure—of love, forgiveness, and patience, or (at the very least) it is the result of poor judgment in choosing a difficult partner in the first place.
>
> —Gary Thomas, *Sacred Marriage*

When you got married you literally signed a contract. You swore a verbal oath to one another in front of witnesses. If you are a person of faith, you made a covenant with and in front of almighty God. If you are not a person of faith, you at the very least made a pact with the state that you would uphold certain vows that you recited publicly. Those vows probably included staying together in a permanent union ("till death do us part"), a promise of sexual fidelity ("forsaking all others"), financial support ("with all my worldly goods I do thee endow"), and emotional support ("to love, honor, and cherish").

Take a look at your marriage vows and see if you are following the agreement you made with each other. If not, you are violating the terms of your contract. While the state may not take actions against you, at the very least, violating those vows speaks to the quality of your character. Additionally, the Bible unequivocally states that God hates divorce. As a Christian you might have some 'splainin' to do someday.

Marriage also grows you as a person. The challenges of marriage grow and mature us both as couples and as individuals. Those challenges make life worth living; having no challenges in life is boring. But people have a propensity to avoid difficulties. So some people leave a marriage when it gets too hard. This tendency of humans to avoid unpleasantness and difficulty keeps us from growing to a higher spiritual and maturity plateau. Persevering through difficulties (of any kind) in life and marriage helps develop our character and make us less selfish. As a man, I've found that marriage has grown me immeasurably. I'm not sure many men are capable of overcoming their self-serving nature without the benefit of marriage.

But your marriage is not just about you. Your marriage is important to many others besides you and your spouse. Certainly your children think your marriage matters (don't be fooled by pop culture—divorce devastates children, even when they are grown). Both your parents and your spouse's parents think your marriage is important. But others are affected by what happens in your marriage as well. This concept struck me a few years ago. I had an epiphany that after three decades of being married, our marriage was not just about us anymore. The truth is that if we were to divorce, it would impact the lives of many other people. Of course we would each be wounded by its fracturing. And our children and grandchildren, yes, but also all of the people who look to us for hope and encouragement as an example that a love can last a lifetime. Should we fold, all the young couples we have mentored and counseled would be highly discouraged and question the advice we had given them. Perhaps even people who have benefited from reading my books or from being involved in our ministry would doubt the veracity of our work. What about all the people who don't actually *know* us but know that we have been married for a long time? Would our demise impact them at all? Maybe it would remove just a bit of hope and encouragement from their own marriages.

Young couples today yearn for stable marriages, but are anxious about the likelihood of achieving it themselves.

Lastly, what about the effect on society our breakup would have? Our divorce probably wouldn't shake the foundations of society, but get *enough* people of all ages divorcing, remarrying, having multiple blended and extended families and it becomes confusing. So confusing that since 1990 the federal government has stopped producing information on marriages and divorces in this country.[4] And where do individual and societal expenses begin and end for struggling broken families in areas such as health insurance, education, and welfare assistance? Not to mention the impact on society resulting from fatherless boys and girls wreaking havoc in areas such as higher rates of crime, promiscuity, and out-of-wedlock children.

Experts believe that divorce is contagious. But so are good marriages. Marriage matters—yours and mine. At the very least it is a stabilizing force for a culture to grow and develop from.

Why Marriage Is Good for You

Eighty-six percent of unhappily married people who stick it out find that, five years later, their marriages were happier, rating very happy or quite happy.

—L. J. Waite and M. Gallagher, *The Case for Marriage*

Permissive divorce laws have encouraged a rise in divorces over the years. The implementation of no-fault divorce laws in the early 1970s appears to coincide with significantly higher levels of divorce in the United States. When United States divorce laws underwent major changes, the divorce rate more than doubled in all states.[5] In 1968 about 25 percent of all marriages ended in divorce. Today that number has doubled, with nearly 50 percent of all marriages ending in divorce.[6] The average length of a marriage is between seven and eight years.[7]

But now our culture is actively promoting the message that divorce is not bad, and in fact marriage might not even be good. It is becoming politically incorrect to even use the word "marriage."

I recently spoke at a conference attended by managers of various state-run social service agencies. Even though everyone in attendance recognized and admitted the significant advantages and benefits of marriage (and many even worked in programs designed to promote marriage among their clientele), they still were cautious about promoting it publically. They somewhat tongue-in-cheek referred to it as the "M" word. It was unfashionable (or at least politically incorrect) to even say out loud the word "marriage" at this conference!

There's a rather silly thought going around today about people looking for someone to marry to "complete" them. Well, that may be true, just not the way most people think. If nothing else, it creates unrealistic expectations in a marriage. Your spouse isn't a ready-made piece designed to add to your pleasure and fulfillment. Your spouse is, however, designed to cause you to struggle and grow into a more "complete" version of yourself than you would have been without them. It is a process designed to force you and your spouse to grow separately and together. At that point (usually after many years) your marriage becomes a completer version of an entity where *together* you are closer to God than either of you would have been on your own.

But beyond all that, your marriage is important, especially for your kids. Children need both the complementary parenting styles of a mother (nurturing) and a father (authoritative) in order to thrive. These love styles (performance-based and unconditional) help teach children character traits and life lessons they need in order to be successful human beings.

One of the biggest myths of our culture is that divorce is the best thing for children when a marriage becomes unhappy—that staying married for the "kids' sake" is a mistake. Divorce may or may not be the best thing for an individual parent seeking their own self-fulfillment, but it's certainly not for children. While children in high-conflict homes may be better off when parents separate, most children (even those in unhappy low-conflict homes whose parents stay together and work out their problems) fare better when both parents are in the home.[8]

A wide range of research shows that children from single-parent homes fare far more poorly than their counterparts from two-parent families in virtually every measurable outcome. Unfortunately, according to vital-statistics data from the Centers for Disease Control and Prevention, 41 percent of all births are now a result of nonmarital childbearing.[9] Here are a few examples of how children fare more poorly in these situations:

- Children in father-absent homes are five times more likely to be poor and ten times as likely to be extremely poor than children living with a mother and a father.
- Children from single-parent homes are much more likely to be neglected and sexually, psychologically, and emotionally abused than their two-parent counterparts.
- Teenagers from single-parent homes were one and a half to twotimes more at risk for illegal drug use than teens from intact homes.

- Boys fourteen to twenty-two years of age who grow up outside intact families are twice as likely to end up in jail. Every year a boy spends living without a father increases the odds of future incarceration by 5 percent. A boy born to an unwed mother is two and a half times more likely to end up in prison than boys raised in two-parent homes.

- Separation or frequent transitions (divorce, new partners, etc.) increase a girl's risk of early menarche, sexual activity, and pregnancy. Women whose parents separated early in life experience twice the risk of early menstruation, more than four times the risk of early sexual intercourse, and two and a half times higher risk of early pregnancy compared to women in intact families. The longer a woman lived with both parents, the lower her risk of early reproductive development and sexual activity (fewer encounters and less sexual partners).

- On average, educational achievement in children from one-parent homes is significantly lower. Children from single-parent homes score lower on tests and have lower grade point averages than those from two-parent, biological families. Children from one-parent homes are more than twice as likely to drop out of school as children from two-parent homes. Additionally, nearly all educational outcomes (grade point average, test scores, achievement tests, and high school/college graduation) are, on average, lower in students from single-parent homes than students from intact families.[10]

Businesses, corporations, and even the government are rightfully concerned about the status of marriages in this country. According to *The Taxpayer Costs of Divorce and Unwed Childbearing—First-Ever Estimate for Nation and*

All Fifty States (2008), family fragmentation (divorce, separation, children born out of wedlock, etc.) costs United States taxpayers at least $112 billion each year.[11] The average employee loses 168 hours of work time the year following a divorce.[12] Absenteeism, reduction in productivity, and increased healthcare costs related to marital distress cost United States businesses and industry an estimated $6. 8 billion per year.[13]

Smart businesses realize the impact home life has on productivity and take steps to provide help to employees in these areas whenever possible. Even the military understands the relationship between a stable home life and the efficient productivity of their members. Several workshops based on my books have been used successfully by these and other entities to help their employees have happier and healthier relationships at home, which then translates into better job performance and productivity.

Husbands and wives provide each other with companionship, sex, and partnership, but also provide a veritable insurance policy in that should something unexpected happen, there is another person to take care of them. If you become disabled, sick, or infirm, there is a person to stand with you and help you through the crisis, a benefit you might not get as readily from a cohabitating situation. Should you die, your spouse will get social security or life insurance benefits, as well as all your worldly goods.[14]

Marriage positively contributes to each individual on a personal level and to society in general as a whole. Your marriage matters to you personally, to others around you, and to our culture in general. Keep an eye on the bigger picture and you'll know that your marriage and those of everyone you know are important.

Now let's look at some practical tips to making your marriage successful and fulfilling. One challenge that most couples face is effectively communicating with one another, which leads us to our second chapter.

Intimacy-Building Tips for Your Marriage

- Pick one night a week to spend together. This could be a formal date, or it could be just spending the evening watching a movie together at home. Time together translates into intimacy.
- Share with each other (and your children) what first attracted you to your spouse. Tell your children (and grandchildren) the story of how you met. Share when and how you knew your spouse was "the one." Sharing stories like these frequently not only reminds you of why you married your spouse, it also gives your children guidelines on finding the right person to marry.
- If you've been married longer than twenty years, renew your vows. Have a ceremony where you recommit to one another. What an awesome event for friends and family! Make it a fun party.
- Pray together with your spouse every day. Prayer is the most intimate activity you can do with another person.

2

Communicating
with the Other Sex

That Is All You Need to Know!

Being heard is so close to being loved that
for the average person, they are almost
indistinguishable.

—David Augsburger

If you ask a man what his favorite thing to do is, I can
almost guarantee you that "talking" or "communicating" won't make his Top Ten list. Even just mentioning
the word "communication" causes most men to either get
nervous or start looking for chores to do.

And then there are women. Who knows what they need or
want? Half the time *they* don't even know what they want.
How is a man supposed to read their minds and figure out what

they want? Then they get mad at you when you don't intuit what they need. Just the opposite of men, they crave conversation and seek it from friends and lovers. Without effective communication, how can a woman ever get her needs met?

Couples with successful, longtime marriages generally rate communication as one of the keys to a happy relationship. But given the inherent differences in the way males and females express themselves, how can a couple reasonably expect to effectively communicate with one another?

A scene from *Jeremiah Johnson* depicts classic poor communciation. After teaching his new Native American wife one English word—"yes"—they have their first conversation:

Jeremiah [points to himself]: Great hunter, yes?
Swan [blank look]: Yes.
Jeremiah: Fine figure of a man, yes?
Swan: Yes.
Jeremiah: Good. That is all you need to know.[1]

To communicate means to exchange or convey information that is received and understood by another. This information can be conveyed in any number of ways—verbally, written, through body language, symbols, or behavior (even pheromones can send signals that are easily understood by another). A business or organization cannot function without effective communication, and neither can a marriage.

Words

You only think I guessed wrong! That's what's so funny! I switched glasses when your back was turned! Ha ha! You fool! You fell victim to one of the classic blunders! The most famous is "Never get involved in a land war in Asia," but only slightly less well-known is this: "Never go in against a Sicilian when death is on the line"! Ha hahahahahaha! Ha hahahahahaha! Ha haha . . .

—Vizzini in *Princess Bride*

That quote doesn't have anything to do with what's in this chapter, I just like it. If you're a guy, you probably do as well. It's a classic line (a bunch of words) from the movie *Princess Bride*. One of the more striking parts of the movie is the communication between soon-to-be-princess Buttercup and farm boy Westley. At the beginning of the movie she imperiously orders him around every day, telling him what to do, and all he says is, "As you wish."

That's either a very wise response or a very lazy one. Regardless, it seems like it would be easier to communicate with a woman that way than to go to all the trouble to actually talk to her. Carrying on an extended conversation often seems more draining and difficult to a man than chopping a cord of wood.

Women like words—at least they use a lot of them. Words don't have the same importance to men as they do to women. Words *do* have great meaning to women though, and when a man speaks the words a woman wants to hear, she longs to believe them. Perhaps that's why being lied to is so egregious an offense to a woman—although the right words can make her forgive and forget pretty quickly. In fact, she's likely not to forgive if the right words aren't spoken.

Men are more apt to judge a man by his actions than his words. Conversely women tend to believe what a man *says* even over his actions. If you don't think women are suckers for words from men, just check out the visitors' rooms at any prison.

Men will often say anything if they think it will get them what they want or, better yet, get a woman off their back. It doesn't mean they really believe what they are saying. Men tend to have short-term vision regarding words—they use words that will solve the problem in the short term without considering the longer term ramifications. Most of the time a man—especially in the heat of the moment—will say whatever pops into his head. If we men truly understood the value that women place on the words we speak to them, we might be more responsible regarding what comes out of our mouths. At least that way we wouldn't be apologizing all the time. This belief women have in the value of words is why they are so wounded by lies. Many women have a difficult time forgiving a man for lying to her, when men typically feel like they were just telling her what she wanted to hear.

Good Communication Traits

> Communication is thus the blood of marriage that carries vital oxygen into the heart of our romance.
>
> —Gary Thomas, *Sacred Marriage*

Good communication makes people feel like they are understood. It allows people to get their needs met. All humans, no matter how young or old, want to feel like they are understood. Unfortunately most people frequently feel misunderstood. Most people don't care about your opinion. They just want you to hear and understand what they have to say.

Customer service representatives apply this strategy when fielding complaints. They want to make a customer feel heard and understood. The goal is to take the heat out of the situation. When I was the manager of a large manufacturing company, I sometimes had to speak with important account customers who were upset. After listening to the person's complaint, I might say something like, "I understand what you are saying. I appreciate your feelings. If that happened to me, I'd probably feel the same. How can I help resolve this situation to your satisfaction? "No matter how upset, nine times out of ten, the customer (or employee) would calm down and we would have a rational discussion on resolving the issue. Even if I couldn't give them whatever they wanted, they generally left our conversation feeling satisfied and still a customer.

Obviously, we shouldn't use a customer service script on our spouse during an argument, but it is still an effective strategy in showing them that we care and understand what they are saying. One way we can make our spouse feel heard and understood is to respond to them in ways that make them feel valued. Generally, men need admiration and respect while women need to be loved and cherished. Both just want to feel heard and understood.

When a woman gives her husband honor, respect, and admiration, she gives him the power to do the things God wants him to do. Yes, it's a lot easier if he deserves that kind of treatment. But what if he doesn't? What if he's just an average guy stumbling through life trying to keep his head above water? He's doing the best he can, but frankly, he's pretty clueless. Does he still deserve your respect? Or worse still, what if he's stupid and doing hurtful things? How in the world does a woman show respect and admiration to a man like that?

Cherishing a woman and giving her the love that she craves can help her blossom into a lovely and luscious version of the fruit that God designed as Eve. But how does a man cherish a woman who demeans him or is contemptuous of him?

Good communication takes time together. As busy as most people's schedules are, it's no wonder we struggle communicating with each other. Spouses in healthy marriages understand the need to go on dates frequently and to take a weekend getaway with each other on a consistent basis (at least once or twice a year).

Most people who come from dysfunctional families don't know what normal communication looks like. Each summer our Better Dads organization hosts a "Foundations in Life" family camp for single moms and their children. We bring about twenty to twenty-five single moms and their children together for a free three-day camp. During the camp we bring out a bunch of men to basically play with the kids all day. This serves to give them the masculine attention and essence they crave, as well as to show them a positive male role model (which many have never seen before). We hold classes for the moms. At lunch and dinner everyone comes back together to share and reconnect. We were surprised when, during the debriefing after our first camp, the moms told us that the thing that was most impactful for them and their children was watching the volunteer married couples interact with each other at meal time. They stated that neither they nor their children ever get the opportunity to see healthy couples relate to each other, and so this was extremely appreciated. We began to intentionally use married couples as our volunteers at future camps.

One year, my wife and I got into a rather heated "discussion" about something silly in front of the lunch crowd. We finally resolved our issues and apologized to each other.

Afterward I thought we had really blown it—some role models we were. But the moms said, no, it was very instructional for them to see a couple express themselves, then resolve their disagreements in a healthy manner. It wasn't something most of them had experienced before.

Of course I then tried to convince the moms that our argument was actually staged for that purpose. But they weren't buying it. The lesson in all this for me was that I didn't think anyone was really paying attention (I thought we kept our discussion pretty contained), but you can rest assured the moms and the kids were watching us like hawks. The same goes with you and your spouse if you have children—there are little eyes always closely watching you both, learning how a man and woman communicate with each other. And they are internalizing the examples that are modeled for them, which they are then likely to mimic in their relationships when they get older.

Bad Communication Habits

> I was searching for the proper word of apology for my outburst against her, but the words fluttered into my head like a colony of luna moths, in disorderly, undecipherable array. I longed for the day when I could say what I meant to say and at the precise time the thoughts came to me, but it was not today.
>
> —Pat Conroy, *South of Broad*

We can develop bad communication habits, which make it difficult for our message to be received and understood. The first bad habit is expecting our spouse to know what we mean, without being specific. Women might be more apt to fall into this trap than men because they expect men to just know what they mean. However, I somewhat frequently tell Suzanne something that I am sure is clear and concise (to me) and she interprets it in a completely different way. Some of that is probably just the innate differences between the sexes and some of it is probably poor communication skills on my part.

When we have this attitude of expecting our spouse to understand, there is no way that our message can be effectively received—it puts your spouse in a no-win situation. And if your spouse does understand, they get no credit (because, after all, they *should* understand); the sender does not feel identified with, nor does the receiver feel validated. If the receiver does not understand the message, he or she may be accused of many things, like being ignorant, intentionally obtuse, or not caring. To combat this, I've developed the habit of politely asking Suzanne to repeat back to me what she thinks I said. This requires me to not be preoccupied when I talk to her though. Suzanne has realized that, since I am a man, she needs to be very specific (even somewhat blunt) about what she wants as well as how and when she wants it.

A second challenge to communication comes in the form of accusing your spouse of something. When we accuse our spouse all the time—for real or perceived faults—it causes that person to become defensive and shut down. Our spouse might think, *Why should I even try to understand when I am being accused of being a bad person even when I'm not?* Couples often get into the habit of jumping to a conclusion. To stop this practice, try not passing judgment upon each other until you gather all the facts. You "conclusion jumpers" out there will soon find out just how difficult this can be.

Similar to accusing is blaming. Blaming someone (especially if that person is innocent) causes the person to question your love and wonder if you really care for him. Imagine what it feels like to be wrong no matter what the circumstance. Would that make you feel loved and valued? I don't mind taking the blame when I legitimately mess up, but I sure don't feel good when I'm unfairly targeted. Again, this is often a habit that one spouse or the other falls into. Like all habits it requires intentionality and diligence to break. A good beginning is to recognize your behavior, admit it to your spouse, then ask for forgiveness. Tell them you are going to try to break this habit (if for no other reason than you don't like being that kind of person) and ask them to bear with you as it will require some time to complete. Then as you slip up into old patterns occasionally (and you will), be prepared to admit it and apologize. I find if I apologize enough times for something, I usually end up changing that behavior, but maybe that's just me. It's humbling, but effective.

Using generalities such as "You always" or "You never" is counterproductive to effective communication. The truth is that no one ever *always* or *never* does something. When you use generalities, you lose credibility with the point you are trying to make. I know about this because, to be frank, I've been known to use a generality or two at times. The truth is, I'm never always right or never always wrong, and neither is my wife.

Criticizing is extremely destructive to your personal relationships, and yet I see spouses (and parents) do this more than any other poor communication habit. Unfortunately, the people who are the closest to you—and therefore should be your greatest champions—are often the people who say the cruelest things. I choose to believe that it's their own insecurities, anger, or pain they are trying to mask, and not a reflection upon me. I also recognize that in our culture blaming someone else absolves you of your problems or your guilt. Therefore I know the person who is lashing out at me is probably feeling guilty about the very thing for which he or she is attacking me. Does knowing that stop me from getting defensive or striking back? Probably not very often, but it does help me understand the factors leading up to the disagreement when I reflect upon it later. That's also not to say that every time my wife gets mad at me it's her problem. More often than not, I'm to blame. But, especially when dealing with wounded or broken people, realizing they may be acting out of their own insecurities makes it easier to understand where they are coming from instead of taking what they say personally.

I have a list of items on my printer that I am forced to look at many times throughout the day. Some items are positive goals that I want to attain. But one of the biggest items is that I want to be a less cynical, more optimistic, and more positive kind of person. Hopefully just being reminded of that every day is helping to change my behavior.

A highly destructive communication habit is expressing contempt for the other person. Contempt is a form of hate or disgust with someone. I think women are more often contemptuous of their husbands than vice versa, but regardless of who is at fault, this trait hurts your spouse and your relationship in general. I've noticed women on Facebook who post a daily list of things they are grateful for. This seems like a great way to change contemptuous behavior, whether you are male or female. Gratefulness appears to be the antithesis of contempt. Also, I know from experience that when I pray daily and thank God for my blessings, I tend to have more gratitude and am less contemptuous of my life and my spouse.

Getting defensive immediately anytime something is said to you also causes the other person to quit communicating. Yes, again I can speak to this trait rather intimately. Being defensive means that you do not validate the message that is being sent, causing your spouse to feel misunderstood and probably frustrated if not downright angry. I believe that if we habitually act defensive when confronted with something, it means we are trying to shift the blame from us to the other person. Frankly, even if we are *not* to blame in the situation, getting defensive makes us *look* guilty anyway. Maybe the best way to break this habit is to not take everything personally.

Also, using the "silent" treatment, or refusing to talk with your spouse, is extremely destructive. Contrary to the name, *silent* isn't a lack of communication; it's a powerful, hurtful form of communication. You are treating your spouse like he or she does not exist. I finally had to recognize that ultimately this was very childish behavior.

Giving your spouse unsolicited advice is a bad habit to acquire. Unsolicited advice is much harder to take than advice that is asked for (there is a difference). If you are peeved at your spouse, it's not a good time to be giving advice. Ask yourself whether or not this information could be helpful or productive. If not, think twice before offering it.

People who are emotionally healthy understand themselves and generally feel understood and accepted by their partner. Unhealthy people don't understand themselves or have a false view of themselves, their lives, and their experiences. In this scenario the issue isn't one of bad communication, it's that their partner can't understand them the way they want because self-perception is distorted from reality. We often get mad when someone won't "accept us the way we are." But if you look at yourself with a distorted view and then demand to be validated, you're asking that your spouse validate an inaccurate representation. That is not only confusing but also compromises our integrity as a person. This is unfair to your spouse and destructive to your relationship.

We know one woman who firmly believes she is the mentally healthiest person walking the face of the earth. Unfortunately she has a ton of issues she hasn't dealt with that cause her to have a skewed perspective on life. She is always upset that her husband won't "accept me for who I am." Yet who *she* thinks she is varies wildly from the way everyone else sees her.

Lastly, being negative is a terrible habit. I know because I struggle with always seeing the glass half empty. Thankfully my wife is a "glass half full" kind of gal, and so she frequently helps me see the bright side of situations. Being around a negative person is just flat draining (I don't even like myself sometimes). And negativity tends to spread rapidly. A negative player on a ball team can infect the entire team. Same with a marriage—negativity affects the entire family. I seem to be wired to be the kind of guy who can find the problem or what can go wrong with just about any situation or project. Sometimes that's a really good trait to have (except when brainstorming) because it saves me a lot of wasted energy trying things that won't work. But often it makes people I really appreciate feel less than empowered. I've had to learn to help people understand that what I am doing is my way of helping them as opposed to being negative—or maybe I'm just being defensive about the whole thing.

If you are guilty of any of the habits described above, can I ask you to consider challenging yourself to change? If you do, you'll find the communication in your marriage change almost immediately, not to mention your relationship will begin to thrive and grow once more.

How Women Communicate

If you beat around the bush, he's going to keep being the bush.

—Sharideth Smith

Even when males and females use the same words, their meanings may be different. Take, for instance, male time and female time. When I ask my wife how long until she's ready to go someplace, she'll often say, "Oh, about five minutes." Five minutes to me means five one-minute (sixty-second) increments on a clock. But in female time that really means, "It's gonna be awhile, buddy. I'm just throwing a number out to pacify you." I always ask my wife or daughter whether the time frame they are speaking of is male or female time. I've come to understand that female time does not always match the numbers on a clock.

Or what about when a wife asks her husband to complete a chore or task around the house. He generally responds with something like, "I'll get right on it" or "I'm working on it." Six months later the chore is still not done and she's wondering how to motivate him to finish it in a reasonable time frame.

All that notwithstanding, women have a fundamental need to be listened to. They equate being listened to with their value and worth. When a man listens to his wife, he communicates that she is worth his time and attention. So many wives (and daughters) tell me they feel extremely loved when their husband (or father) gives them his *undivided* attention.

A woman's tongue has the power of life or death. She can infuse life into a man or stab him to his knees merely by the words she chooses to speak into him. More important may be *how* she says them to him. Spiteful and contemptuous women cut men into pieces with rapier-like precision, using words they wield like a scalpel. But women who use this power wisely can empower men to feats of greatness, merely with a few well-chosen words.

Not all communication requires words. Body language oftentimes conveys messages even more powerfully than a woman's words. A raised eyebrow, a well-timed sniff, an eye-roll, arms akimbo on her hips, toe tapping, or arms tightly crossed over her chest all send precise messages. Every husband in America knows how his wife feels just by listening to her in the kitchen. If she's humming, all is well. If she's slamming pots and pans around muttering to herself, well . . . a storm is brewing.

Men, we all know (or should know) by now that a woman doesn't necessarily want you to fix her problems when she talks about them. She shares them with you as a way to process them and to draw closer to you emotionally. She doesn't need your advice, but she really needs you to *care*.

However, ladies, if you don't tell him what you need, he won't know. Many women think, "If my husband really loved me, he would just know what I need." But that's not how a man's brain is wired. His thinking is linear and he doesn't fill in gaps very well. Therefore he tends to not be able to read minds or even read between the lines of a conversation. It doesn't mean he doesn't love you or care about you, it just means he can't think like a female. Trust me, he *wants* to fulfill your needs—it empowers him as a man. He just often doesn't know how or even know what your needs are. So you want him to know what you need? Be specific—tell him bluntly and succinctly. We need crystal clarity on what you want. We do poorly at interpreting what you *meant* to say. Men appreciate conversation that cuts to the chase and gets to the point.

And men, if you don't express yourself (at all), how can we expect her to know what we mean, what you need, or how to satisfy our needs? We men tend to not feel comfortable expressing ourselves, yet we get resentful when our wives do not meet our needs. While she does have superior communicative skills, it doesn't mean she can intuit unspoken thoughts. She cannot read our minds—even though it seems that way sometimes.

How Men Communicate

> As I grow older, I pay less attention to what men say. I just watch what they do.
>
> —Andrew Carnegie

I was speaking at a conference of mental health professionals (almost all of whom were women) on how to communicate with males—specifically younger males. I was explaining that because males have shorter attention spans, female counselors needed to get to their point sooner and use fewer words. In addition, the women needed to stick to one topic at a time during the course of a conversation.

One woman raised her hand and said, "I think it would be disrespectful to my husband to talk to him like that. It would almost be like talking down to him." I asked the two men attending the workshop their opinion. One said, "It would be very refreshing to have a woman speak to me like that." The other said, "I can only dream that my wife and female co-workers would speak that way to me." I suggested to the woman that she was interpreting communication through her filter and not through a male's. Likely, a woman *would* feel disrespected if you spoke to her in short, simple sentences.

Because of the way a man's brain is wired, it takes longer for the average male to process information and to decide what he is feeling, especially when multiple concepts are involved in an emotional context. It makes sense a male would prefer simplicity when you communicate with him.

It's important to understand that the way males and females are predisposed to communicate is neither right nor wrong—it's just different. Understanding those differences allows us to create effective strategies to communicate better. Since, in general, females are superior wordsmiths, they tend to be better at developing effective strategies to communicate with the men in their lives.

Men's brains have the ability to compartmentalize things. That is why they can go off to war, experience horrible circumstances, and then come home and live relatively normal lives. Or why they can be arguing one minute and ready for sex the next. Or why they can't do two things at once. Because of the way their brains are wired, men struggle with multitasking. I can't even sign a book and talk at the same time.

As if to underscore this point, I'd spoken at a conference one evening and the next morning, my wife and I were having breakfast at the lodge where we were staying. Our male waiter was pouring water into our glasses when my wife said to him,

"Are you ready to take our order?" To which our waiter very deliberately replied, "No, ma'am, just a moment please."

When he finished pouring each of our waters, he put the pitcher down, looked my wife in the eye, smiled, and said, "Okay, what would you like?"

Clearly he had learned not to try to do two things at once. He was very effective at pouring water or at taking our order, but he couldn't do both things at once—at least not proficiently.

I was recently giving a father-daughter presentation. After my talk to the fathers, they engaged in a number of bonding exercises with their little girls. One of those exercises was to teach the fathers to "fix" their daughter's hair. A hairstylist was brought in to give the dads some simple tips on styling hair and they were turned loose to make the most creative hairstyles possible, with the winners being judged later. Being competitive, these men were *intensely* focused on performing a task that most of them had never accomplished before. As they worked on getting their thick fingers to perform skills beyond their normal capacity (perfectly forming braids and finger curls), the female counselors encouraged the dads (without much success), "Tell your daughter what you are thinking about!" I finally had to tell these well-intentioned ladies that the men *couldn't* tell their daughters their feelings. They could only concentrate on learning an unfamiliar task.

The male brain's inability to process what's said and then to respond as quickly as the female brain means that men struggle to communicate verbally during stressful situations. It's why they tend to get angry if they have trouble expressing themselves during arguments.

Because males do not perform as well as females in verbal encounters (and males are very performance-based), men frequently hesitate to engage in emotional topics or to talk through problems. But, guys, remember this, *ignoring unpleasant issues or repeatedly avoiding them always causes them to fester and eventually erodes your marriage.* Many marriages operate under a low-grade fever of discontentment or anger. Contentment in your marriage is not a result of the absence of problems—contentment comes through effectively resolving those problems when they appear. Every marriage is going to have problems. This is why good communication is an essential part of a healthy marriage. But ineffective communication can create problems that were not originally there.

Arguing

> Joe didn't want to fight either. Every time they did, he lost, found himself apologizing for things he hadn't even done, hadn't even thought of doing, found himself apologizing for not doing them, for not thinking of doing them. It hurt his _____ head.
>
> —Dennis LeHane, *Live by Night*

A lawyer once told me that arguing with a woman is like getting arrested—everything you say can and will be used against you. So if men are smart, they use their right to be silent. Unfortunately, that strategy can lead to more problems than it solves.

It seems like every time my wife and I are going somewhere to speak on the topic of marriage, we end up getting in a big fight on the way. Ever had that happen? Most people experience frustration in communicating with people of the opposite sex. Put two people together for years on end and it can magnify issues pretty quickly. Many people divorce and use "irreconcilable differences" as the reason. My wife and I have had irreconcilable differences with each other for the past thirty-two years. We just figure it comes with the territory.

Most people think conflict within marriage is the sign of a troubled relationship. But in fact, conflict can be healthy. Conflict often leads to growth in individuals and couples. Marriages without conflict are dead or headed for trouble. Author Gary Thomas says it this way: "The absence of conflict demonstrates that either the relationship isn't important enough to fight over or that both individuals are too insecure to risk disagreement."[2]

My friend, pastor's wife and author Susie Davis, shared one of her experiences:

> Like Easter weekend. What should have been a grand, glorious heaven-on-earth sort of weekend was absolutely crappy for us. We got in a big, huge, confusing fight (we were both ridiculous) and did that barely speaking, stare down thing you do when you're mad at your spouse. It was super wonderful and spiritual. . . . Some twenty-four hours later when we were just too tired to keep up all the anger and defensiveness, we exhaled. And then we talked. Like professional married people. People who aren't going anywhere no matter how stupid crazy they act.[3]

"Professional married people." What a unique way to look at your marriage relationship. Most of us tend to lash out to protect ourselves when we feel threatened. But if I keep a viewpoint of being a "professional" married person, perhaps I can control that knee-jerk response and not feel the need to snap at my spouse.

One study shows that the average married couple only talks to each other about twenty-seven minutes a week. The most words exchanged between couples is on the third date and during the year before they get divorced (probably because they are fighting so much).[4] That amount of time doesn't seem adequate enough to nurture an intimate relationship, much less express all your needs and desires.

An elderly pastor once told me, "If you are going to argue, argue naked." Great advice. I just wish he had told my wife instead of me, because she didn't think it was very funny that I dropped my pants whenever she got mad at me. But I digress . . .

Sometimes people pick fights with their spouse just to get a reaction. It lets them know that person is still there. Particularly if communication is bad or nonexistent, people who are too dependent upon their spouse might feel more secure from the pressure and tension of disagreements. It doesn't make sense on the surface, but for some people any contact (even negative) is better than no contact at all.

Other people (generally because of unresolved wounds) are always "on guard." They never relax—they're always ready to do battle with anything that comes across their emotional radar screen. Being constantly tense (ready to go to battle) exerts too much emotional energy and actually provides very little protection. Continually being in that state doesn't leave you much energy left in your emotional bank account to expend in other areas such as loving, caring, or nurturing (yourself or others). Psychologist David Schnarch warns:

> When you are constantly clanking around in your emotional armor, you are a sitting duck for anyone who wants a fight. You can't move quickly because you are stressed out all the

Working through Problems[5]

- *Look at the issue as a personal problem*: If you look at the issue as your personal problem instead of your spouse's problem, you'll lose your puffed-up sense of self-righteousness and won't feel like a victim.
- *Look at the issue from a historical perspective*: If you can't see your part of the problem look at it from a past perspective. Have you faced problems like this in the past with other people? Are you the only common denominator? Maybe you *are* the problem.
- *Stop taking your partner's reaction personally*: Ask yourself why you are getting defensive about your partner's reaction. Don't take it personally—especially if it is a distortion of the truth.
- *Stop working on the idea that you are "working on your relationship" or that "the relationship is the problem"*: "There's something wrong with our relationship" usually means you want to work on your partner's problems. When you work on yourself, you are working on the relationship. When you change, your marriage changes.
- *Stop focusing on what your partner is (or isn't) doing*: Focusing on yourself indirectly increases the pressure on your partner to change.
- *Stop trying to change your partner*: Pressuring your partner to change actually reduces the pressure on both of you to change. If your partner thinks you are trying to drag him in your direction, it will make it easier for him to "dig his heels in" and resist or be complacent.

time. You keep your radar going full strength, but you can't see anything new. Being tense offers little protection, increases your vulnerability, gives a false sense of security, and increases your reactivity.[6]

The more you are able to control your emotions (calm yourself) the more stable the relationship and the less you are controlled by your spouse's emotions and anxieties. When we expect our spouse to shield us from anxiety and insecurity, we are placing undue stress on our marriage. It's not your spouse's job to protect you from your own insecurities—it's your job to deal with them as part of the contribution to your relationship. If we take it out on our partner whenever we are angry and expect them to reassure us, we exhaust the emotional bank account of our marriage. Our partner eventually loses patience along with the ability (and desire) to soothe us.[7]

And for heaven's sake, if you can't regulate your emotions, at least try to control your behavior. We often compound problems by creating chaos around us when the problem is actually within us. If that means you have to physically remove yourself from the situation to control saying something you'll regret, so be it.

Or as well-known radio host Dr. Laura said, "Just because a thought crosses your mind, don't assume it should come through your lips. Where did you ever get the notion that free speech meant you didn't have to consider appropriate restraint when dealing with the feelings of a beloved or the well-being of the entire family?"[8]

There's an old acronym in the mental health field called SHALT. It's said that you should never argue with your spouse when you experience SHALT. SHALT stands for Sick, Hungry, Angry, Lonely, and Tired. All of those feelings cause us to escalate and intensify our disagreements. For instance, when I am hungry I get "hangry"—I get hungry and angry. If you try to discuss something with me when I have the "hangers," I'll likely bite your head off. But let me eat a snack and I'm all ears.

I also think it is important to never name-call during an argument. I know several couples who call each other horrible names when they argue. Yes, some have stayed married, but it always seems to me to be so disrespectful to one another. I'm not sure how these couples can be intimate with each other after spewing that kind of hate onto each other (how do you make love to someone who just called you a horrible name?). The words we speak often influence our thoughts, which then influence our feelings. Calling each other vile names always places a negative feeling toward them in our brain and on our heart.

A positive strategy to use which will actually prevent arguments is the 7 Cs. The 7 Cs were first introduced in 1952 by a professor named Scott M. Cutlip, in his book about public relations. They are generally used in marketing, but who knows more about how to quickly get their point across than someone trying to sell you something? The 7 Cs consist of being Clear, Concise, Concrete, Correct, Coherent, Complete, and Courteous! Use these and you should be able to get your point across to your partner without offending them, even when talking about the most delicate of topics.

Some couples feel like their marriage is stuck—it's not going anywhere. Many times when couples experience gridlock (where one partner wants to change and the other doesn't) or even when they are chafing against one another, they believe they are having problems in their marriage. In truth, that's just part of the growth process. None of us experience growth in the exact same time frame. Usually when this happens we try to find a detour around the problem instead of facing it head-on. The point is that sometimes problems are good—not bad. It means there is still some passion in the relationship. The problem is worse when neither spouse cares enough anymore to get upset.

One thing that makes working through our issues in marriage difficult is that people seldom have an accurate view of their own life. We tend to minimize (or exaggerate) experiences (probably as part of our coping mechanism). For instance, for many years I minimized the impact of growing up in an alcoholic home—I "stuffed" the issue and stated "it was no big deal." Well, unfortunately, it was a big deal. By ignoring it I just caused the problems to fester and get bigger when they finally did come out (and they always do). I minimized it so I could avoid dealing with the impact of it because it was painful.

One thing to keep in mind that will probably stop a lot of arguments: It's not your job to "fix" your spouse. It's your job to fix yourself. Be the best person you can be despite whatever kind of person your spouse chooses to be.

Change is hard and growth is often painful. We tend to avoid pain whenever possible. It takes a lot of courage to intentionally try to deal with issues that are painful to us. In order to have a healthy marriage, we need to have healthy streams of communication. That allows us to grow together instead of apart. And so we need to have the courage to address issues that will probably cause us pain if we are to grow.

But most of us will fight having to take too close a look at ourselves. For instance, many a woman likes to promote the fallacy that she wants a man to be able to talk to her about anything—to share his heart with her. She likes this scenario until a man talks about something bothering him about *her*—such as her weight gain or her appearance. Then somehow he is being insensitive and hurtful. She quickly manipulates the situation so that she is the victim and responds with punitive (or hysterical) measures. A man finally gives up, stuffs his concerns, and shuts down. If she won't talk about things that are important to him, why should he talk about things that are important to her? Then his woman complains that he won't talk to her. But he knows he doesn't have the skills to converse at her level, so why try when it's just likely to generate denial, anger, tears, or (worst of all) loss of sex.[9]

Remember that words spoken in anger cannot be taken back—they stay in the hearts of those who receive them. The Bible talks about capturing your thoughts and being slow to speak. In multiple passages it refers to the power that the human tongue has to damage or uplift other people. With that much power comes great responsibility. Use that power wisely.

Intimacy-Building Tips for Communicating with Your Spouse

- Put on your spouse's shoes. Try role reversal occasionally. Have a conversation where you communicate with each other in the language of your spouse. *Note:* This should be lighthearted, not intense. This is a fun exercise to try in small groups.
- Review the section on Bad Communication Habits in this chapter. Rate yourself on habits you want to improve upon. If you have the courage, allow your spouse to rate you as well. Make sure you share with your spouse the good communication habits they have that you appreciate about them.
- Sit down with your spouse and pick one topic you want to talk about. Then have each spouse use the 7 Cs to state their position as shortly and concisely as possible. Be sure to have the other spouse repeat back what they thought they heard you say.

3

Love

Under the Moon and Stars
We Did Meet

Being deeply loved by someone gives you
strength, while loving someone deeply gives
you courage.

—Lao Tzu

Love is a deep affection or romantic attachment to something or someone. Beyond that, love consists of traits such as unselfishness, loyalty, devotion, tenderness, passion, and compassion. True love is sacrificial even to the point of death. I don't know any parent who wouldn't give their life in exchange for their child's (and probably their spouse's as well).

Part of the fun of a long-term relationship (of any kind) is the growing together through shared experiences, suffering together through difficulties and heartbreaks, and experiencing the joy of mountaintop encounters together. But getting through the challenges of life as a couple requires us to have a long-range view of love and marriage. If we don't keep our eye on the bigger picture, we will get distracted by all the inconsequential and inconvenient problems that crop up in life. These distract us from the larger vision of what's really important.

I continually have to remind the young couples my wife and I mentor to keep their eye on the big picture. When you do that, many of the small problems and irksome habits of your spouse become less significant (or at least bearable). For instance, sometimes the amount of attention young children require can cause a young mother to focus on the children as the center of her world. In that role she is invaluable. But a long-term vision remembers that you and your husband will be together long after your children have grown and moved on. That vision will help her to balance her attention on both her children and her husband. Likewise, men need to remember that work is just a means to support their family. Yes, we get satisfaction from our accomplishments, but later in life your work will be one of the *least* important things you care about. What will matter most is your family. I remember hearing that advice when I was a young man and thinking, "Yeah, sure." Now I can tell you—it is the truth.

Falling in love is the easy part. But staying in love takes work and intentionality.

Teamwork

Every marriage moves either toward enhancing one another's glory or toward degrading each other.

—Dan Allender and Tremper Longman III

Think of your marriage as a team unit, not two individuals. Then remember that you are on the same team. Sometimes during the heated battles of life we start looking at our spouse as the enemy. It's important to give your spouse the benefit of the doubt in most situations. Always look for the best in your spouse. Too often we attach negative motives to our partner's actions and responses. But in all likelihood your spouse has your best interests at heart. Your spouse cares about you (probably more than anyone else in the world does) and only wants the best for you. Sometimes it doesn't feel that way, but I promise you if you communicate that to your spouse, your spouse *will* reciprocate, believing you want their best too.

The other thing to remember is that a marriage is a living, breathing vessel. It has a life of its own independent of you or your spouse. It ebbs and flows. It has seasons—good seasons, bad seasons, and even indifferent seasons. There will be times when things are rough. It seems like the rough times will last forever. The truth is, they are just a season—they last at most a year or so, probably less. It just seems like they last longer. Seasons of trials are often followed by seasons of joy and blessings. These seem to last for shorter periods, but when you weigh everything out over a long period, they tend to last just as long as the difficult times.

Think of it like the professional baseball season that consists of 162 games and lasts from April to October. There will be times when a batter goes through a slump. He can't buy a hit. Then there are times when it seems like he can swing at the ball with his eyes closed and get a hit every time he steps to the plate. I'm guessing the slumps feel like they last longer, but over an entire season they even out.

When I became a full-time writer and speaker, it took over six long years of financial struggle before we gained some stability. Those were very lean and difficult years that we struggled through together. I can tell you though that those struggles have been followed by several years now of great joy and blessing. It is so much richer a blessing because we persevered through those trials. The same is true of your marriage. There will be lean times that you will walk through together. Once those pass, a season of blessing and joy will follow. The problem is, we tend not to remember the times of blessing. Struggles seem to stay in our memories longer.

Try this experiment. Sit down with your spouse and try to remember the difficult times of your marriage. Chances are you'll be able to recall pretty clearly all the tough times you've had (at least your wife will). Now write down what the root cause of those struggles was. It's important to reflect back on our challenges and understand what caused them, especially if you do not want to repeat them. Was it finances? Was a child sick or rebelling? Perhaps old wounds arose and needed to be dealt with. Once you agree about what the cause of the struggles were, now discuss what solved them. This is important too. Understanding how we weathered specific issues can help us in the future during similar situations.

Now try to remember the period that followed, after the problem was resolved. Chances are your marriage went through a time of happiness and maybe even prosperity. Like many problems in life, once we endure and persevere through them, we end up getting blessed for our efforts. The point here is to remember the good times and not just the bad ones. Love is shaped and grown by going through life's challenges together. There is something about persevering through difficult circumstances that builds character in ourselves and in our marriage. Those who cut and run at the first sign of difficulty never get to experience the joy of standing together on the mountaintop, arm in arm, knowing that you can truly depend on the person beside you.

What Could Go Wrong?

Love must be learned, and learned again and again and again; there is no end to it. Hate needs no instruction, but waits only to be provoked.

—Katherine Anne Porter

No one falls in love because it's the smart, practical thing to do. One of the more tragic love stories of the Bible is that of David and Michal. After slaying Goliath, David became famous—a brave and handsome young man admired by many. This made King Saul jealous and he decided to try to kill David. After finding out that his youngest daughter Michal was in love with David, Saul offered to give David her hand in marriage. In an attempt to get others to do his dirty work for him, Saul then proposed that David bring him 100 foreskins of the Philistines as payment for his daughter's hand—something he figured would surely get David killed trying to accomplish (given the fact that those were something the Philistines were pretty intent upon keeping). In typical David fashion, he returned and presented Saul with not just 100, but 200 Philistine foreskins and Saul had no choice but to allow him to wed Michal (1 Sam. 18:20–27).

Nothing is said in the Bible about David's feelings for Michal, but clearly she loved him dearly. At one point when Saul was coming to kill him, she warned David to leave and then deceived the guards into thinking he was in bed ill in order to give David time to get away (1 Sam. 19:11–17). As David remained a fugitive, Saul gave Michal to another man (Paltiel) in marriage, either as punishment for her deception or just to get even with David (1 Sam. 25:44). After Saul was killed and David became king, he eventually bartered with his enemies to get Michal back.

The Bible doesn't say how long David and Michal were separated, but her new husband wept when she was taken away. David apparently hadn't gone to any great lengths to try to rescue her, and she may have fallen out of love with David by that point. For whatever reason, Michal soon developed feelings of contempt for him. Later, when David brought the ark of the covenant into the city, wearing a short sleeveless linen garment, he joyfully led the procession "leaping and dancing before the LORD." As Michal watched him from her window it says, "She despised him in her heart" (2 Sam. 6:16). That's a pretty strong statement of a wife's feelings toward her husband. The following passages document as heated and bitter an exchange between the two as any argument that couples engage in today:

> When David returned home to bless his household, Michal daughter of Saul came out to meet him and said [sarcastically], "How the king of Israel has distinguished himself today, going around half-naked in full view of the slave girls of his servants as any vulgar fellow would!" (2 Sam. 6:20)

David said (indignantly) to Michal,

> It was before the LORD, who chose me rather than your father or anyone from his house when he appointed me ruler over the LORD's people Israel—I will celebrate before the LORD.

I will become even more undignified than this, and I will be humiliated in my own eyes. But by these slave girls you spoke of, I will be held in honor. (2 Sam. 6:21–22)

And then comes a verse that is one of the saddest I've ever read and speaks volumes about the future they shared together: "And Michal daughter of Saul had no children to the day of her death" (2 Sam. 6:23).

We don't know if Michal was jealous of David dancing partially clothed in front of the slave girls or if she felt his behavior was beneath the dignity a king should exhibit and reflected poorly on her. Regardless, her scorn and contempt of David led to a relationship that did not produce any children (perhaps as punishment for her pride or because they did not sleep together again). Clearly Michal did not have the relationship she wanted, and her love for David, once so promising, soon wilted like an unwatered flower.

This also brings up an interesting point regarding today's relationships. The expectations, attitudes, unresolved wounds, and unfulfilled needs of each partner can severely damage your marriage. If any of those desires are not expressed, they cannot be met, and resentment soon creeps in to your relationship.

The one thing that most contributes to a husband's satisfaction is his wife's contentment. Because of that he will instinctively assume responsibility for her happiness, and she often lets him. But if he finds that he cannot make her happy, he will eventually quit trying. Nothing is more demoralizing to a man than to have a wife who is constantly complaining and criticizing him.

On the other hand, a wife who uses her powerful words to uplift a man empowers him to accomplishments he could

How to Divorce Proof Your Marriage[1]

1. Make your marriage your highest priority.
2. Learn good communication tools.
3. Attend a marriage workshop.
4. Get help early. The longer you wait, the harder it will be to repair.
5. Stop your own negative behaviors.
6. Keep your sexual relationship alive.
7. Make regular deposits into your relationship account. Do kind and caring things every day.

never achieve on his own. As a wife, are you taking responsibility for your own happiness? Are you using your power positively or negatively?

Likewise when a man abdicates all of his leadership roles within the home, it also causes problems. A marriage with a dominating wife usually has an unhappy, insecure woman and a frustrated and unfulfilled man. Assuming the main leadership role in the relationship means she acquires the masculine characteristics that accompany leadership. Being forced to lead and make all the decisions, she soon realizes she has lost some of her feminine charm, which is as important to her as masculinity is to a man. The hurt is compounded when she realizes it is the fault of her husband's deficiencies. He is less of a man in her eyes. His wife loses respect for him because of his loss of manliness, which causes her love for him to diminish.[2]

Men, are you leading your wife and family or do you hand the reins to your wife and stand by and watch as she gets frustrated and angry trying to handle *all* the details of life? Do you allow her criticism (potential or actual) to keep you from even attempting to lead? What would happen if you shocked your wife and stepped forward and assumed your God-given leadership role in the family?

Additionally, men who abandon their families place them in extremely difficult positions. Working with single mothers and fatherless boys, I've seen too many cases where the husband established his career while the wife sacrificially bore and cared for his children, only to have him take off with another woman, leaving his wife with the responsibility of raising the kids by herself. These women and children are generally poverty stricken and destitute. I know a lot of men who did not want to get divorced, but those men who intentionally abandon their families should be ashamed of themselves.

I'm not condemning you if you've been divorced (certainly there are justifiable reasons for divorce and you can't control the actions of another), but I am encouraging you to try to persevere through a difficult marriage. Not a marriage with serial infidelity or abuse, but one that is difficult. Maybe communication is poor, you're having problems in the bedroom, or you're just plain fed up with your spouse for a variety of reasons. Sometimes just letting your spouse know you are committed and won't cut and run because things are tough is enough to encourage them to change their attitude.

The truth is that happiness cannot be the sole determining factor in whether or not we stay married. If happiness alone were the most important factor in marriage, we'd all need to get remarried every couple of years. That's about how long the hormones last that give us a "high" every time we enter into a new relationship.

Unfortunately, many women "settle" for a man and then want to change him. A woman cannot change a man, but she does have the power to make a man want to change from his natural self-centered, egocentric nature into one who is willing to make sacrifices for others.

I have no idea what my wife saw in me. I was an angry, broken young man from an abusive alcoholic home. I drank booze, did drugs, and smoked cigarettes, for crying out loud. How could she possibly have seen anything in me that would have led her to believe that I would make at least a marginally good husband, provider, and father? And yet, it worked out for her. I'm not the best husband, but I'm not the worst choice she could have made either. Obviously I stopped all those behaviors long ago and channeled my energies into more productive activities like work and education. But how could she have known that I wouldn't follow in the destructive footsteps that were modeled for me while growing up? Being in love and getting married forces us to face some character issues we might otherwise never choose to face.

A good woman often brings out the potential in a man. Loving a woman inspires a man to want to be better, achieve more, and earn her pride and respect. I know plenty of situations where I thought a man didn't have much going for him, but after a few years of his woman by his side, he hit his stride and became very successful. And I've seen it work with women as well. Many women bloom under the loving guidance of a good man.

Women have an incredible power through their relationships to effect changes in the world around them. Gary Thomas, in his wonderful book *Sacred Marriage*, says,

> God acts in many ways like a woman. Women are capable of and sometimes commit magnificent acts that manifest incredible power and awaken in us men a profound awe, if not fear and trembling. Yet when they love, they love quietly; they speak, as it were, in whispers, and we have to listen carefully,

attentively, to hear their words of love and to know them. Isn't God also this way?[3]

If you've ever truly loved a woman, or been loved by a woman, you know that statement rings true.

How to Keep Things Right

> Immature love says: "I love you because I need you." Mature love says: "I need you because I love you."
>
> —Erich Fromm, *The Art of Loving*

Good, loving relationships don't just happen. They take time, patience, and hard work in order to grow and prosper. Everyone experiences challenges in marriage (your problems aren't as unique as you think they are). Those who are successful learn effective strategies to deal with problems. Just understanding that men and women are different in almost every way is a good first step to having realistic expectations from your spouse.

As a culture we place too much emphasis on the *emotion* of love and not enough on the *action* of love. Sure, for the first few months (or even first couple of years) after meeting someone, hormones are coursing through our bodies, creating a high that makes us giddy and allows us to overlook the idiosyncrasies in our partner that will later drive us crazy. But once those wear off and our body stops producing drugs in such huge quantities, how do we maintain a loving relationship?

Our culture promotes the romantic notion of love being about feelings and that our feelings then dictate our actions. It describes love as a passive emotion; we have "fallen" in love, we were "swept off our feet," or we "couldn't help ourselves."

8 Tips from the
World's Happiest Couples[4]

1. *Kindness helps*: 74 percent of couples who said they were happy give each other back rubs.
2. *It's not necessarily about the looks*: 20 percent of the happiest partners say they're not physically attracted to their spouse.
3. *Similar personalities help*: Of the 45 percent of people who say they have a lot in common with their spouses, 95 percent describe their relationships as extremely happy.
4. *Keep talking*: 40 percent of the happiest couples say communication—more than friendship, affection, or even sex—is the most satisfying part of the relationship.
5. *Avoid the couch*: Only 1 percent of the happiest couples say they've ever slept on the couch.
6. *Some secrets are OK*: 27 percent of the happiest couples have kept secrets from each other.
7. *Be intimate often*: 60 percent of extremely happy couples have sex three or four times per week.
8. *Arguing can be healthy*: 78 percent of the happiest couples argue occasionally.

However, love is an action, a verb, not an emotion. We choose to love someone and we choose to take the actions that keep that love alive. We *choose* to invest in our relationship or choose to let it die.

Love is more about what we *do* than how we *feel*. Frankly, sometimes I don't feel like doing loving things for my wife (and I'm sure she feels the same about me). But surprisingly, when I force myself to do those things, I always feel more love for her. She in turn feels more love for me because I have acted lovingly toward her. It's an interesting cycle, in that our disciplined thoughts lead to actions, our actions then lead to feelings.

Also, as a culture we have an unrealistic perspective of what love looks like. We think someone in love is always happy and filled with romantic bliss. But you can love someone and still dislike or even hate them occasionally. Just as you can hate someone and still love them—like a child's feelings toward an abusive parent. Emotions are seldom either/or—they are complicated. Emotions are often conflicting. Just because you are ambivalent about your spouse from time to time doesn't mean your marriage is over. We all go through seasons in any long-term relationship when we don't like the other person or are tired of them. But because our culture tells us (primarily through movies and women's magazines) that love looks like romantic bliss and constant happiness, the first time we enter a season where we are dissatisfied or even disdainful toward our spouse, we automatically think the marriage is over and it's time to move on. Not true. In reality it is a normal function of life and it just means our relationship is following a normal course of growth and development. Often that "falling out of love" phase we enter is the beginning of a new growth cycle that allows us to discover true love and deeper intimacy, which is impossible when chemicals (hormones) are interfering with our thoughts and feelings.

If you're honest, there are times when you are pretty sick and tired of your children. It doesn't mean you ditch them and find new ones. Why would you do that with your spouse? Obviously, I'm not talking about an abusive situation, but sometimes it seems as if married people would rather be unhappy than happy. In fact it's easier to be unhappy than it is happy. It requires more effort to become happy and to maintain happiness than it does to give up and succumb to discontent and misery. I see people every day (and you do too) who seem to relish living lives of disappointment and dissatisfaction. And they enjoy spreading that gloom to the world around them.

Our own attitude has a lot to do with how happy we are in marriage (and in life). If we choose to be content and satisfied, then we will tend to be happy and content. If we choose to be critical and negative, we'll probably be miserable—and so will our spouse. A successful marriage requires both partners to respect each other. The challenge is that we have to honor our spouse even when we know his or her deepest character flaws.

In his book *Creating an Intimate Marriage*, counselor, radio host, and author Jim Burns talks about creating a marriage based on *affection*, *warmth*, and *encouragement* (AWE). He believes that if you choose to live a life filled with AWE (despite however your spouse responds), you will not be forced to "live a life based on circumstances or reactions to your spouse. It is a decision to proactively live a life filled with self-control in which you choose to set an atmosphere that leads your relationship to a healthier spot."[5]

Even a much loved, considerate partner will profoundly disappoint you at times. Truthfully, we are spoiled. We have been given more of everything than any previous generation in the history of the earth and yet we are still unhappy. Like petulant children we want more and more despite being given everything we could ever need. Our relationships show it.

Loving someone takes a lot of courage. To truly open your heart up to someone is to be vulnerable to being hurt. The *more* you love them, the greater the chances of being deeply hurt. I suspect many people hold back for that very reason—they are scared of being deeply hurt. Or perhaps they have risked their hearts before and have been deeply wounded.

Part of the problem may also lie in the fact that people today are more self-focused than past generations. For instance, according to the National Institutes of Health, the incidence of narcissistic personality disorder is three times higher among twentysomethings than among those over sixty-five. You might be able to explain that away as their maturity level—except that the average college student in 2009 scored significantly higher on a narcissism scale than his counterparts did in 1982. And the high self-regard doesn't end when they graduate; 40 percent of all Millennials (born early 1980s to early 2000s) believe that they should be promoted every two years regardless of their actual job performance. Most troubling of all are their ideas about right and wrong. "The guiding morality of 60 percent of Millennials in any situation is that they'll just be able to *feel* what's right."[6] In other words they have no moral foundation to base decisions upon other than their feelings—which are notoriously fickle judges of right and wrong.

Having high levels of narcissistic tendencies combined with using emotions (as opposed to principles) as a guide is the very definition of a marriage heading for divorce. It is difficult to love others if you do not love yourself. But being *in* love with yourself presents a whole new set of problems. It's hard to love someone else when you are too busy showering love upon yourself. It's one of the challenges we find in parenting teenagers; they tend to be extremely self-focused. They don't care about the needs of anyone else.

Interestingly, though, feelings play a big role in a woman's life, even if she's not narcissistic. One of the biggest things a woman needs is consideration for her feelings and desires. A man can validate or invalidate his wife by how he accepts her feelings. Her need to express resentments, troubles, and concerns and then have a husband give them genuine consideration is significant.

I have a bad habit of getting impatient every time Suzanne brings a concern to me. Frankly it seems like she brings a lot of concerns to me. But that is one of her ways of expressing her needs and staying intimate with me. It's also her way of making sure I am aware of important things. Past experience has taught her that I can be distracted or not aware of things around the house that need my attention (like a leaking ceiling or a broken garbage disposal). My wife needs me to be available and willing to support her by listening to her as she processes issues such as relationships challenges she is facing or even internal dilemmas she is dealing with. By acting as a sounding board, I am actually developing intimacy with her.

As men we cannot always solve a woman's problems, and she probably doesn't want us to. But what she does want is for us to listen, try to understand, and sympathize. Ultimately she wants to know that we love her and would take away the hurts, injustices, and exhaustion of life for her if possible.[7]

Isn't that what everyone wants?

Intimacy-Building Tips for Loving Your Spouse

- Sit down with your spouse and recall some of the difficult times of your marriage. Now write down what the root cause of those struggles was. It's important to reflect back on your challenges and understand what caused them, especially if you do not want to repeat them. Once you agree about what the cause of the struggles was, discuss what solved them. Next, try to remember the period that followed, after the problem was resolved. Chances are your marriage went through a time of happiness and maybe even prosperity. The point here is to remember the good times of your love life and not just the bad ones.

- Tell your spouse five things you "love" about them. Better yet, write them down on a note and put it someplace it will surprise them (bathroom mirror, briefcase, refrigerator, etc.). Do this at least several times a year.
- Tell your wife you love her every day and tell her why. Tell your husband why you respect and appreciate him at least once a week.
- Go on a romantic getaway at least once a year. This is not your annual vacation but a special quick little rendezvous weekend with just your spouse.

4

Romance and Intimacy

The Soul of a Marriage

I love you not only for what you are, but for
what I am when I am with you.

—Elizabeth Barrett Browning

Guess which chapter of this book was most difficult for
me to write? You're right—this one. While I understand intellectually the concept of romance and the
importance it has in a woman's life, I don't really understand
it psychologically. I don't *get* it. But I do know that romance
is an essential part of a loving relationship for a woman.
Therefore, we men have to make a conscious decision to try
to meet this need whether we understand it or not.

And intimacy . . . well, let's just say it's not my strongest
trait. If I'm being honest, the only time I intentionally get

close to being intimate is during sex or those rare moments when my wife and I connect on a deeper metaphysical level. I accidently have episodes of intimate behavior, but in general it makes me pretty uncomfortable. Intimacy requires us to lower our guard, exposing our innermost being. It requires us to be vulnerable, which is diametrically opposed to the way a man typically functions. I was raised with the "old school" admonitions that a man was stoic, endured pain quietly, and did not show his emotions.

And yet, without romance and intimacy our marriages are cold and boring. Lack of romance and intimacy shrivels our wives like succulent roses left in the scorching heat of the unrelenting sun in the desert of a passionless heart. Men who do not intimately and romantically pursue their wives become apathetic, complacent, and overly involved in work or hobbies.

You can be assured that, as a writer, I will always be challenged in the exact areas I am writing about. I've had many epiphanies and challenges while writing this book.

After working hard and traveling a great deal for many months, I realized while writing this chapter that I had been neglecting this area of my relationship with my wife. I could see her starting to "wilt on the vine," so to speak. So I took an entire weekend and planned time together with her. On a sunny Saturday morning, we walked to the local farmers' market and shopped for fresh produce (and fresh-cut flowers). That evening I took her to a Barn Bash. This longtime local event includes all-you-can-eat BBQ and live music. Hundreds of people attend this event each year. As we arrived amid the swirling activity and noisy buzz of people having a good time out on the town, my wife was transformed into a much younger woman. Her countenance was excited and there was a tremor in her voice as she looked around with a sparkle in her eyes. We spent a fun-filled evening together reconnecting and enjoying each other's company.

The next morning I took her to the largest antiques and collectibles show west of the Mississippi. We spent over six hours looking at every item known to woman (most of it junk to my mind). But she was thrilled! To her, that kind of an adventure is close to the gates of heaven. To me it's more like Dante's ninth circle of hell. Frankly, it was grueling. But I soldiered on and kept a good attitude with a smile on my face because I knew how important it was to her. She was clearly in her element talking with everyone she met and touching every item in each booth. As a reward for my endurance, I did learn about a number of things I never would have known before, such as the history of dental chairs and calendar art, what the steampunk movement is all about, and how to properly shoe a horse like an old-time blacksmith.

Plus we were blessed to meet Karolyn Grimes, the woman who played the littlest daughter Zuzu in the movie *It's a Wonderful Life*. She was a very classy and fascinating lady who told us many stories about Jimmy Stewart, Frank Capra, John Ford, and John Wayne. She also worked alongside famous actors like Cary Grant, Loretta Young, Maureen O'Hara, and Bing Crosby. As we left, Suzanne remarked, "That's a woman I'd like to invite out to dinner sometime." I wish she would have said that before we left, because I would have!

On our way home, Suzanne was so appreciative of my spending the weekend with her that she couldn't stop chattering about it. She remarked contentedly, "The best part was, I had your undivided attention. I had you all to myself."

While I didn't really do anything other than be "available" and intentional in the time I spent with her, the weekend spoke intimacy and romance into her heart. My taking a small amount of time to plan some things that she was interested in and then "dating" her the entire weekend told her I loved and treasured her.

Passion isn't just something that floats around and lands on your head like a snowflake. It needs to be tended and nurtured. Otherwise your marriage gets tedious and the fire dies. The embers of passion blink out and only the cold ashes of a once roaring fire are left. As the flames of your early passion die down, you need to bank the coals and turn them into a forge—one that provides life-giving warmth for a long time.

Most of this chapter will be directed toward men, because if you are anything like me, this is the area of marriage you'll have the most trouble fulfilling your wife's need for. Why? Because it seems unnatural to our male character and the way we are designed. But once you see the importance to your wife and some ways to help you meet those needs, you too will be blessed with a happy (if talkative) woman on your hands.

Romance

> A couple can never drift together; you can only ever drift apart. And unless you're intentional, you will drift!
>
> —Sheila Wray Gregoire

I frequently tell women to be very choosy when seeking a husband. I encourage them not to "settle" for the first man who comes along and tells them things they need and want to hear. Make sure he has a good work ethic, strong moral character, and treats his parents and those who are weaker than he is and can be of no benefit to him with understanding and compassion.

My advice for most men is much simpler—if you can find a woman who will put up with you, marry her. No, seriously, if a woman makes you want to conquer the world, that's a pretty good indication that she's "the one." Being in love with a woman means you are willing to do all those silly things outside your comfort zone to woo her. You stay up late talking all night, hang on her every word, agree to do things (like ice skating and dancing) that you'd never do if you were in a sane state of mind. It also means you are willing to spend the emotional energy, money, and time to romance her heart. Unfortunately, after we win her heart we tend to revert back to our previous nature. That's like sitting out the rest of the game after playing a great first quarter. Marriage is a long race. The initial courtship is just the opening sprint.

While men appear to dread a female's concept of romance, most men will tell you they actually enjoy romance. It's just that a male's idea of romance differs from a female's perspective. The female idea of romance usually involves a male performing in public, which is frightening to most men. It might involve dancing in front of people, proclaiming your love publicly, writing and reading poetry that doesn't even rhyme, or surprising her with some unexpected yet fantastic gift or preplanned trip. All of those activities put a man at risk for failing or looking ridiculous (especially bad if it's in front of other people). Additionally, it can be difficult to anticipate what a woman considers romantic. She might think your efforts are silly or even pathetic. And once criticized, many men will never attempt a romantic gesture again.

Dating after you are married is an extremely important part of keeping your relationship alive and vibrant. Interestingly men consider doing things together or playing together as romance. They feel that companionship is romantic and enjoy just spending time with their wife. Because most men are action-oriented, doing things (not talking about things) is far more satisfying than cuddling on the couch and whispering in each other's ear. They derive great satisfaction through the companionship of their wife. Taking walks together, going hiking, going to the game together, or even going golfing together are all activities a man might find romantic.

Women, on the other hand, don't often view simply spending time together as romantic. The other day my wife mentioned that we were not dating enough. I protested, "What do you mean? We've been doing all kinds of stuff together!" I figured we had been dating nearly every day—we'd been going to some really cool places together. But she responded, "That's not dating, that's just going places together." Her expectation was that it would involve a more formal process of asking her on a date, getting dressed up, and then going somewhere more romantic than the muscle car show or food court.

Also men feel like sex is part of romance. To be romantic and not culminate in having sex feels somehow incomplete to a male. Whereas for women, romance is appreciated in and for itself. A romantic time may culminate in sex, but it doesn't have to. Most men are highly disappointed in that attitude.

Perhaps because dating and courtship are so easy and fun, we are lulled into a false sense of security that marriage will be just as easy. We become complacent. When we first meet, dating is so fun—you connect with that person, you love spending all evening talking, you relate to that person on a

The 10 Commitments[1]

1. Each morning when I get up, I will tell my wife I love her and she's beautiful.
2. Each day at work I will call my wife at least once and let her know I'm thinking about her.
3. I will not flirt with any women I meet during the day.
4. At the end of each day, I will leave the problems of work at work. At home, I will commit to being cheerful, positive, and engaged.
5. When I get home from work, I will kiss my wife on the lips for fifteen seconds.
6. Each evening I will ask my wife about her day and then actively listen as she talks.
7. I will speak to my wife as I would an honored guest in my home.
8. Each week I will be willing to do one chore for my wife.
9. Each week I will give my wife one special treat that she enjoys and that communicates love to her.
10. Each year I will take one special weekend away with my wife.

visceral level, you wake up excited to see them later that day. We act that way because hormones are racing through our system—we are actually on drugs!

After we get married, our attention turns to other issues. Part of the challenge with many marriages is that they become "child-focused" instead of "spouse-focused." Each partner puts their children's needs ahead of their spouse's. Author and radio host Jim Burns contends, "What we don't realize is that child-centered marriages are often weak marriages, and in the long run they hurt the kids more than help them. If your spouse is not getting his or her emotional needs met by you, often he or she will pour all their energy into the children. The end result is an unhealthy marriage relationship."[2]

> ## 5 Romantic Needs of a Woman[3]
>
> - To be spiritually ministered to by her man
> - To feel safe and secure with her husband
> - To share intimate conversation
> - To receive a tender touch and hear gentle words
> - To be pursued and set apart by her man

It's important to court your wife. I'll admit that I'm not the most romantic guy on the face of the planet. But I at least make an attempt (when I can rally myself out of the recliner).

I would even say that the more chaotic and hectic your life is, the more you need an established date night each week. Busy at work? Kids driving you crazy? Don't feel like dating your spouse because you're too stressed? Too bad— go on a date with your spouse anyway. That's the time you need to date your spouse the most! It doesn't have to be expensive. Take the kids to Grandma's for a couple of hours and go sit in the park and talk. Or just lie next to each other on the grass and look up at the stars. Even going to a coffeehouse and sharing a hot cocoa on a winter's night can be an opportunity to reconnect and nurture your relationship. Find other couples to trade off children on each other's date nights.

What you don't want to do is have a marriage fail and look back with regret that if you had just not gotten complacent and had put a little more effort into appreciating your spouse, the marriage and your family could have been saved.

Intimacy

Everyone has a desperate need to be loved. Everyone also wants to be wanted and needs to be needed. But oftentimes we hold back from wanting, needing, or even loving our spouse—at least on a deeper level. Our spouse is just as desperate to trust and to love someone and to have someone love them in return. We hold back because to love or need or want *too* deeply is to run the risk of being rejected, and no one wants to be rejected. It hurts too badly. The deeper we want or need someone, the deeper the rejection. We all fear rejection and so we emotionally withdraw when we begin to get too close to someone. To be wanted too deeply gives that person (your spouse) power, leverage, even importance in the relationship. So we hold back—we don't dare to love too deeply for fear of being hurt, or controlled, or taken advantage of.

Young couples today are especially susceptible to this emotional restraint. Psychologist and author Dr. Laura Schlessinger says,

> With so many of their parents divorcing—often multiple times—young people are afraid of hurt and loss so they "play" with intimacy without really risking much in the hope that they can create "safe love," only to discover that such a situation doesn't exist and that they feel desperately lonely.[4]

Intimacy is about letting yourself go—becoming vulnerable enough to allow yourself to be *known* to your spouse. Intimacy ebbs and flows throughout an ongoing relationship—sometimes becoming richly deeper and other times shallow and cold. Young couples reading this might think, *I don't want a marriage that is shallow and cold!* But that is normal occasionally. You cannot run passionately hot continuously—you will burn up!

Some of you reading this might think your marriage is too far gone to change. But the old saying "it takes two" doesn't apply here. It takes two to keep your marriage the same; it only takes *one* to change it.[5]

Part of becoming intimate with your spouse involves touching. The human skin is a very sensitive organ. Touching each other generates feelings of calmness, lowers stress, and creates intimacy between two people. A warm touch releases the wellness hormone oxytocin and reduces levels of the stress hormone cortisol, prompting people to feel better and be more cooperative.[6] Studies have shown that hand-holding actually creates physical intimacy among married couples and even lowers blood pressure and reduces stress in hospital patients.[7]

A pastor friend of mine started a program several years ago here in the Pacific Northwest called Compassion Connect. Their objective is focused on offering free health care and other service resources to the uninsured, underinsured, and homeless community of Portland. It is their mission to bring healing and transformation through compassionate service to the community. They do this by gathering hundreds of volunteers, including medical and dental professionals, hairstylists, and other community service providers, and basically providing free medical and dental services on site that this community does not normally have access to. They host dozens of these events around the Western states, serving tens of thousands of people.

Frequently I will serve at a booth that provides education regarding the fatherhood programs that I am involved with. At the last event our booth was next to the haircutting area. I noticed that the hair stylists were cutting the homeless people's hair using their bare hands (with no rubber gloves). At first, I'm ashamed to say, I was a bit repulsed.

But as I watched further an amazing thing happened. The stylists spent as much time rubbing the scalp, petting the hair, and gently caressing the faces of their clients as they did actually cutting their hair. Amazingly, even the most agitated and aggressive clients became very calm and relaxed. Touch had a soothing effect upon them. I realized that what the stylists were doing was giving these people their dignity back by touching them. That small amount of skin-to-skin contact made them feel human again and welcomed them back into the community of people. It was an astonishing illustration of the remarkable power of human touch. Even more remarkable was watching the volunteers wash the homeless people's feet. Many had sores and were filthy. Yet the volunteers, with grace and dignity, knelt and washed their feet while praying for them just as Jesus would have all of us do. The looks of joy and contentment on the faces of the clients were priceless.

The next time you are struggling with your spouse, reach over and take their hand. Guys, maybe even kiss the back of your wife's hand. Better yet hug each other—multiple times a day. That human contact is a better stress reducer than a tranquilizer. Human beings need human touch from another human. Babies who do not get held enough die—it's called Failure to Thrive Syndrome. Don't let your love die from lack of touching one another.

Many people think good communication leads to intimacy—and communication is a part of healthy intimacy. But communication alone does not lead to intimacy. Many couples communicate messages to one another that are very clearly understood but are hard to hear or accept, like angry accusations, criticisms, or complaints. They are communicating very effectively, but they aren't developing intimacy.

Dr. Schnarch elaborates:

Intimacy is often misunderstood as necessarily involving acceptance, validation, and reciprocity from one's partner—because that's what many people want if they're going to disclose important personal information. But intimacy is not the same as closeness, bonding, or caretaking (all of which bring comfort by emphasizing togetherness, continuity, and shared history). Intimacy is an "I-Thou" experience. It involves the inherent awareness that you're separate from your partner, with parts yet to be shared.[8]

In relationships, you get what you give. At some point in your marriage there will be times when one spouse feels like they are giving more than the other. And truthfully there may be people married to an unhealthy spouse who is only capable of taking and not giving. But generally we reap what we sow in relationships. Your marriage is a living entity and needs to be nourished just like your body needs nourishment in order to continue functioning.

There's an old joke that goes like this: Joe had asked Bob to help him out with the deck after work, so Bob went straight over to Joe's place, arriving the same time Joe got home. When they got to the door, Joe went straight to his wife, gave her a hug, and told her how beautiful she was and how much he had missed her at work. When it was time for dinner, he complimented his wife on her cooking, kissed her, and told her how much he loved her.

Once they were working on the deck, Bob told Joe that he was surprised that he fussed so much over his wife. Joe said

Building Greater Intimacy

1. *Affection and caring.* Nonsexual touching, hugs, and kisses are important. If your wife anticipates you want sex when you hug or kiss her, she won't feel intimate. Also, pray for each other. Take time for each other, and show each other love and respect.
2. *Vulnerable communication.* Marriage should be a place where spouses can share anything, including their childhood, their pain, their crazy dreams, their disappointments, their hopes, and anything else in safety. Safe and vulnerable communication is nonjudgmental, and one spouse shouldn't be trying to "fix" the other.
3. *Mutual living.* Intimacy includes a desire for spouses to be together and share their experiences and daily life. Certainly, everyone needs time for solitude or personal hobbies, but there should be an intentional pursuit of enjoying time together. Often love and affection are measured in both the quality and the quantity of time you give.
4. *Mutual giving.* Do you look for ways to please your spouse? Do you seek ways to relieve her stress, to serve her, and make her feel special? Plan special dates with her, and let her know ahead of time so that she can be ready.

that he'd started this about six months ago, it had revived their marriage, and things couldn't be better.

Bob thought he'd give it a go. When he got home, he gave his wife a massive hug, kissed her, and told her that he loved her. His wife burst into tears.

Bob was confused and asked why she was crying. She said, "This is the worst day of my life. First, little Billy fell off his bike and twisted his ankle. Then, the washing machine broke and flooded the laundry room. And now, you come home drunk!"

Clearly, this was a woman bereft of intimacy in her life.

Factors of Concern

> When you go through a valley, it's important to remember
> that it's normal and you will come out of it. Don't overreact.
> Stay the course. The payoffs are well worth it.
>
> —Michele Weiner-Davis

When I grew up, my parents (especially my mother) thought it was great fun to use vicious words, putdowns, and cruel jokes at the expense of another to "win" discussions and disagreements. The person who could criticize or "cut-down" the other the most decisively was a winner and the recipient of praise. But winner and loser both were psychologically cut to shreds by the verbal swordplay (besides, a parent with better communication skills always won). Having grown up this way, I just naturally assumed this was the way normal people related to each other. Imagine my surprise when Suzanne refused to play these sarcastic "games" and in fact insisted they were unhealthy. Of course she was right, but it took awhile for me to understand the damage they do to each person. It took even longer to come to an understanding with my mother regarding appropriate boundaries around my new family.

This type of verbal gamesmanship may have been one reason why my parents' marriage failed. Certain attitudes or behaviors are pretty reliable predictors of divorce. These attitudes include criticism, contempt, invalidation, withdrawal, avoidance, and escalation of negative responses.

Being critical of your spouse does nothing but create negative responses and poor self-esteem. We already know that the words of a spouse have great capacity to either wound or empower. Using those words critically is psychologically the same as abusing someone physically. Name-calling is particularly destructive. Besides, being around negative people is emotionally and physically draining.

Contempt is one step beyond being negative. Being contemptuous of your spouse is similar to hating them. Nothing poisons a person's soul faster than a partner who has contempt for them. Being contemptuous is actively trying to destroy them.

Invalidating your spouse is also highly destructive. It means you think so little of them that nothing they say or do matters or is important.

Withdrawing and avoidance are passive-aggressive behaviors that are nearly as destructive as overt behaviors like being critical and negative. Generally these behaviors signal the end of a relationship. It means the spouse doesn't care enough anymore to even fight back.

Doing all of the behaviors cited above to a child would eventually destroy that child. What do you think it will do to a marriage? Also, what do children learn when they observe this kind of behavior in a marriage?

Another sign of a struggling marriage is when one or both spouses lie to each other. If you are going to have a deeply intimate relationship with someone, you cannot lie. You cannot lie to them—period. Intimacy is built on trust. The very foundation of trust is the knowledge that you can depend on that person to always be truthful. To my knowledge, my wife has never lied to me. It's one of the reasons I like her so much—I know she is not deceitful to me. I never have to question it when she says something to me. I never need to wonder about her motives or if she has a hidden agenda. And I've never knowingly lied to her. Now, it's likely over the years she has omitted saying something or even embellished events in order not to hurt my feelings (I know I have with her occasionally), but there was never malice or deceit in her intent. I trust her. I trust her with everything in my life: finances, parenting, my career, and most of all my heart. How can you possibly trust your heart to someone whom you can't trust to be truthful?

I know several young couples who routinely lie to each other—sometimes over items that don't even need to be lied about! It's clear to me that these couples' marriages are in trouble and doomed to fail if they don't begin trusting one another enough to be truthful.

Also, as we've already discussed, don't try to change your spouse. It won't work and you'll just get frustrated. You probably already know that you cannot change another person— only yourself. I've found when I work on becoming the type of person I want to be (regardless of how my spouse acts), not only am I happier, but oftentimes my spouse changes in response to the changes she sees in me—frequently for the better! If you are frustrated with your relationship, try working on being the kind of person you are proud of and feel good about. That's a proactive response. Otherwise you are allowing another's actions or opinions to dictate how you feel about yourself, which only leads to more frustration and feelings of hopelessness. Besides, it's not your job to fix your spouse—only to fix yourself.

If you or your spouse are trapped in the habit of relating to each other in any of these ways, I encourage you to get into counseling as soon as possible. Recognizing and understanding destructive behaviors is the first step in overcoming them. That's not only healthy for our marriage but for our spouses, our children, and ourselves.

Becoming Your Spouse's Friend

The biggest predictors of a long-term successful marriage are couples who have fun together and those who are friends with each other. Most people (even those in relationships) are starved for emotional closeness and connectedness. While sex is important to a relationship, affection, warmth, and encouragement may be even more important factors to long-term success. Having fun together is one of the biggest ingredients of intimacy in a marriage. One of the strongest traits of healthy families is the ability to *play* together.[9]

In other words, you need to be good friends with your spouse in order to have a healthy, successful marriage. Marriage is a marathon, not a sprint. In order to last for the long haul you have to be friends with your mate or you'll never make it. Do you and your spouse still go to the traveling carnival together? How about something silly like midnight bowling? What about finding other couples to play card games with? Men bond strongest with those they have physical experiences with, and women develop intimacy through experiences with loved ones. *Doing* things together builds friendship and promotes intimacy.

It's important to laugh together and enjoy each other's company. Couples who invest in each other's lives have more satisfying and enjoyable relationships. The times when Suzanne and I are laughing our heads off with each other (usually about something no one else would "get") are the best times of our marriage.

Find other couples to befriend and do things with each other as families. Sometimes it is difficult finding other couples who enjoy the same things and have the same value system as you do, but it's important to have friends to share life with. It's also important for your children to be exposed to other adults and family rituals. These adults can help reinforce the same values in your children that you are trying to establish.

But that said, we need to be careful about the kind of people we hang around with and allow to influence our children. Too many affairs happen between a spouse and the other spouse's best friend.

Qualities that reflect a good relationship include plenty of positive "put-ups" or compliments. In humans it takes upwards of ten affirming comments to offset one critical one. Too often we get in the bad habit of neglecting our spouses when they are the ones we should be most lifting up with our words. I realized one day that while I was making a concerted effort to be the kind of boss who says uplifting comments to his employees, I was virtually ignoring that rule within my own family. Even though it felt somewhat "contrived" at first, I began making an intentional effort to start using my words to lift up my family. It was amazing to see how quickly they responded! They shyly accepted my compliments at first (I suspect they wanted to see if I was sincere), but quickly began to be eager and grateful to receive them as they kept coming. But this is a habit I have to remain vigilant on even today. My wife deserves way more compliments than I give her. I often think nice things about her, but seldom express them as often as I should.

Compassion and Empathy

Happiness comes from being the best person you can be— someone you are proud to be. It cannot depend upon the kind of person our partner is or what they do for us. We attain fulfillment by growing and changing ourselves, not our spouse. Then we are not dependent upon the type of person our spouse chooses to become.

I try to focus on being a better husband rather than wishing I had a better wife. Generally, the type of husband I am reflects back to me in the type of wife I get. When a person is a Christian, they grow by living faithfully for God. The truth is, if I yearn for a different partner, I am absolutely correct—I do need a different partner. But it's not my spouse's fault, it's me. I need to change. When I change, I'll have a new spouse.[10]

When your children are grown and gone from the house, you will either be left with your spouse or be alone. By committing resources to your marriage throughout the child-rearing years, you work toward a relationship you'll both enjoy after the kids leave. Also we cannot control the choices our adult children make. Sometimes they make poor choices or even reject their parents. In those circumstances it's nice to know you have a husband or wife to depend on and stand by your side.

Is it easy to focus on keeping romance alive? No. Is it worth it? Yes!

Intimacy-Building Tips for Romancing Your Spouse

- Hold hands with your spouse every chance you get. Skin on skin contact creates intimacy.
- Hug and kiss your spouse at least three times every day—preferably in front of the kids.
- Be intentional about using words that uplift your spouse every day.
- Set an "unbreakable" date night at least twice a month.

5

Sexuality

Only Women Look Good Naked

Sin will keep a man from talking about his
sexual temptations.
Sin will tempt a woman to be offended by
his sexual temptations.

—Rick Thomas

Sex isn't love. Sex doesn't even necessarily equate to romance or intimacy. You can have sex and not be in love—men and women do it all the time. So just because you sleep with someone does not mean you are in love with them or that they are in love with you. And guys (in case you were wondering), sleeping with a lot of different women does not make you a "man." Ladies, sleeping with a man does not mean he will love you or even cares about you.

Sex is one expression of love, but not the only one. Our culture tends to portray sex as the main component of a romantic and intimate relationship. Movies show people in love having nonstop romantic sexual encounters morning, noon, and night. Perhaps while you are young and unfettered with children that may be a somewhat accurate reflection of your relationship, but try doing that with a couple of babies in tow and see what happens. All of a sudden, if you believe the amount of sex you have indicates whether you're in love or not, you think something is broken. That "romantic sex" thing ain't working so good anymore—at least for a while. (Relax, it comes back.)

Contrary to what our culture promotes, human sexuality is not just about genitalia, or even about having an orgasm. True sex or sexuality occurs only when we have matured enough to have a deep, committed, *intimate* relationship with another person. That typically isn't possible with young or immature individuals.

In fact, we reach our "genital prime" long before we reach our actual sexual prime. Most humans don't really *get* sex or even sometimes enjoy it until they are mature adults. For instance, adolescent males can get an erection and ejaculate quite quickly many times a day, which means they may be in their genital prime, but it doesn't mean they are in their sexual prime. Sexual prime generally happens later in life for most men. We know that adolescent fumbling in the backseats of cars doesn't really qualify as quality sex. If we consider that *real* sex—sex with intimacy—doesn't occur until we have developed deep feelings for someone, then sex with strangers is merely a physical exercise, not a spiritual experience. But the truth is, you don't have to be single to be strangers—many married couples do not know each other well enough to be vulnerable enough to become intimate with each other. Once a couple does become emotionally intimate with each other, a woman does not have to apologize for her sexuality, nor a man for his physical need and desire.[1]

And guess what? Studies show married sex is better than single sex! Despite the stereotype of married people having a boring sex life, research reveals just the opposite. Studies show married couples have almost twice as much sex each week as singles do. Not only that but they enjoy it more than their single counterparts. In a national sex survey, 42 percent of married women found sex extremely emotionally and physically satisfying, compared to just 31 percent of single women. Married men of course rated even higher. Plus both males and females were significantly more likely to remain faithful to their partner if married than if they were just dating or cohabitating.[2] So, want to have a lifetime of good sex? Get married and stay married.

Our sexuality consists of a combination of eroticism, desire/passion/love, and emotional connection. Our sex drive or desire is partially driven by natural causes, such as biological programming (hormones and the drive to procreate), relieving tensions (horniness), and the craving for sexual gratification (libido or sex drive). Additionally, other factors that contribute to our sexual desire (or lack of) include desire for interpersonal communication, bonding, passion (lust and carnality), and cultural expectations (e.g., a woman's bare breasts in the West are sexy but merely pragmatic in African tribes).[3]

Emotional stimulation is nearly always a more powerful sexual stimulant than touch. I hear from many couples who struggle in this area. The causes of their problems are almost always emotional and not physical (our bodies naturally know how to respond if we don't overthink things). Anxiety, bitterness, anger, disrespect, lack of trust, and childhood wounds all transfer into the bedroom and prevent the sex organs from working.

An important thing to remember is that the person with the least desire for sex always controls the sexual climate of the relationship (just like the one with the least desire for intimacy controls the intimacy level of the relationship). With that in mind, let's explore male and female sexuality.

Her Sexuality

> If you haven't seen your wife smile at a traffic cop, you haven't seen her smile her prettiest.
>
> —Kin Hubbard

Recently, I was listening to a local public radio station. The topic was a study on puberty. The study suggested that girls are reaching puberty earlier than ever, sometimes as young as seven or eight years old. While everyone on the panel agreed that early-onset puberty brought with it a number of negative health risks, one guest offered insight into the psychological effects of early puberty that most of us probably do not think about.

One aspect of puberty in females is that many of the physical manifestations of puberty occur before menstruation and the internal feelings of sexual desire. That means a young girl's outward appearance changes before her brain becomes sexual and she desires sexual behavior. But in a society that takes every opportunity to sexualize young women, these young girls learn that their bodies elicit a response from the people around them—the bat of an eye, the movement of their hips, or a coy look. Advertising, television, and movies reinforce the notion that if they act a certain way, they'll get a specific reaction from the men and boys they encounter. Even though they don't feel internal sexual desire, they know that their bodies are having an effect on the people around them. At a very early age girls learn to equate sexuality with performance. The focus is on how they are affecting the audience (especially males) with sexual movement and behavior even though, in one panelist's words, "they aren't developmentally able to connect that to authentic, erotic feelings." They're focused on asking, "What does the audience want of me?" and then trying to give the audience what it wants, before asking, "What do I want?" And they don't know what they want because their internal biology hasn't caught up with their outward appearance and the way in which they are sexualized by clothing companies, cosmetic companies, television shows, and so on.

That discussion opened an entirely new insight for me on how our culture sexualizes girls before they are able to understand what is happening to them. It explains why a lot of women place so much of their self-worth on their looks and whether or not they can attract a man to sleep with them. It also begs the question as to whether women who are sexualized at a young age (which many are—probably more than we care to admit as a society) are capable of understanding their own sexual needs and enjoying a healthy sexuality.

Many women believe there is something wrong with their physical appearance. Because of the influence of the media,

Madison Avenue advertising, and the fashion industry, many girls grow up believing that they are flawed physically and magnify any perceived imperfection they may have. They compare themselves to unrealistic and unattainable standards—the models used in advertising are on some level freaks of nature (plus they are Photoshopped), by no means a typical female. The truth is (and any man will readily admit this) that the female body, due to its curves and proportions, is a work of art just the way God created it. In fact it has been the subject of art since before civilization (even cave paintings glorify the female figure). Perhaps because men are so eager in their approval of the female body, women choose to believe the marketing ploys designed to motivate them to feel inadequate so that they will purchase products or services. Does this affect their sexuality and their sex lives? Undoubtedly.

Sex and Women

For all the talk about men and sex, you'd think females don't like sex. The truth is women enjoy sex just as much (or even more) than men do. They just enjoy it *differently* than most males. One of a woman's greatest needs in sex (those in a relationship anyway) is to know her husband's advances are motivated by genuine love and will be expressed with tenderness and consideration—that she's not just being used to satisfy a physical need. She wants to be wanted for *her*, not just for her body. At least that's what they tell me.

However, some women have been wounded early in life by men they should have been able to trust and whose job it was to protect them from the very acts that they themselves perpetrated upon them. A woman in those circumstances associates guilt, shame, or fear with her sexuality. It is understandable that for these women the ability to trust a man and allow him into the most private places of her heart can be challenging. Other females have had harsh words spoken to them in anger by family, friends, or even other envious women. Those verbal wounds penetrate deep into a woman's psyche and cause her to doubt her beauty and natural sensual potency. These women often struggle with embracing their sexuality and joyfully engaging in an intimate relationship.

In addition, men, if you have been neglecting your wife's feelings, she may not be *able* to respond sexually, even if she wants to. The biggest sex organ of the human body (in both males and females) is the brain. Sexual foreplay for a woman begins early in the morning and lasts all day, and takes the form of loving and cherishing her, respecting and edifying her, understanding her feelings, and appreciating her as a person.

Women have some significant advantages with sex. First of all they are multi-orgasmic. This means they are capable of having multiple orgasms, instead of just one like a male (at least older males). These orgasms might not be as intense in females as in males, but they are not any less enjoyable from what I can determine. However, females generally take longer to achieve orgasm and need greater amounts of foreplay.

Biologically, females are much more complex than males. Trust me, there are all kinds of things I don't know—and don't want to know—about the internal workings of the female body (even though television commercials seem determined to make sure I am privy to every detail). That said, if you want to have a better sex life, understanding how your spouse's body (and yours) works is key to understanding how to satisfy them, and ultimately satisfying yourself.

Since a woman's body is a lot more complicated, start with that. A great many men (all their bragging about exploits aside) know very little about how the female reproductive and sexual organs work. Surprisingly, many women don't even know a lot about that area of their anatomy either, which does not allow them to get their needs met in this area. If you and your spouse are inexperienced or even naive about anatomy, I encourage you to educate yourselves through books on the biological and physiological aspects of the human reproductive system. That might even be another great bonding and friendship-building exercise for spouses!

His Sexuality

If you remember the iconic sitcom *Gilligan's Island,* the age-old question for men of my generation was "Ginger or Mary Ann? " Ginger was the glamorous and voluptuous movie star while Mary Ann wore pigtails, gingham shirts tied at the waist, and blue jeans. Most men would probably rather spend a single night with the seductive Ginger, but prefer to spend a lifetime with the wholesome, girl-next-door Mary Ann. After all, Mary Ann can cook pies. But it speaks to a male's sexual psyche in that the seductress is very alluring, but only for a short time. It's no wonder that most women have an instant dislike for the "Gingers" of the world, but feel less threatened by the "Mary Anns." With that in mind let's look at some "snapshots" of male sexuality.

I admit that I've been somewhat guilty in the past of promoting stereotypes about male sexuality. While most men do think a great deal about sex, very few actually act on those thoughts. For example the vast majority of men, single or married, are not trying to have sex with as many women as they can. College students aside, men are generally happy with one partner at a time and are not really interested in one-night stands. If you think about most of the men you know (fathers, brothers, uncles, friends, co-workers, etc.), you'll realize that the stereotypes of men being sexually aggressive or "thinking with their little head" really only apply to a few of the male gender. While a bachelor may tend to measure his desirability by how many women are attracted to him (want him), most married men are perfectly content with the woman they chose to share their life with.

So when you hear someone say something like, "All men are like that" or "Men are only interested in sex," I would encourage you to challenge them. Ask them, "Really? Are all men like that, or some, or just a few? "If we want to promote healthy male sexuality, we have to break some of the stereotypes that influence the way males are brought up and even think of themselves. A male who hears his entire life that "men are only interested in sex" is brainwashed into believing that women are only good for one thing. They are also more likely to believe that males should look at pornography because "that's what men are interested in."

If we want to produce men who are emotionally aware and sensitive to the needs of others, we have to recognize that they respond to the feedback they receive—positive or negative. Understand that every time a woman berates or criticizes a man publicly for his behavior, it reinforces the notion in every man's mind (at least those within earshot) that it is inappropriate to act that way. If this is used only on bad behaviors, then that's good. But if a woman criticizes a man publicly by calling him a wimp for showing his emotions, perhaps that's not such a good thing for men to hear because it causes them to stuff their emotions.

Sex in Marriage

Sex is like anything else—the more you practice it, the better you get. Young people always think they are better at sex. Trust me, I've been young and now I'm old(er). Old people know a lot more about sex and how things work. You (and my grown children) might not like the image that creates, but older people are just as sexy (or at least as sexual) as young people, only more knowledgeable.

But the truth is that intimacy in marriage is not just about sex. Yes, sex is a big part of marriage (sometimes a REALLY big part), but your sexual relationship will evolve and change just as your marriage does over the years. Anyone who has babies and toddlers running around knows that your sex life changes dramatically from what it was pre-children. You are too tired and worn out to have sex other than a brief, desperate groping in between feedings, baths, and diaper changing. But that too is a season in your marriage and fades into another cycle within a few years. As you and your sex life mature, you become intimate with one another in ways not possible when the eager fervor of youth is thrashing together beneath the sheets.

Part of having intimacy in a long-term sexual relationship is being vulnerable enough to express your likes and dislikes, needs, desires, and even fantasies. Feeling safe enough with your partner to allow them to help fulfill your emotional and physical needs is what true intimacy is about. It takes the willingness to open up and offer a very deep part of yourself to another person and hope they will not crush or reject you. That takes courage. But when couples trust each other enough to become that intimate with each other, sex naturally becomes more fulfilling and satisfying.

When a woman understands that, she can take her marriage to a whole new level. How do you think your husband would respond if you asked him to share his sexual fantasies with you, and then you offered to help him fulfill them? I suspect he'd be ecstatic. Likely, you wouldn't be *able* to fulfill many of them because fantasies are exactly that—fantasies. But just sharing them could be quite exciting. Or maybe it's not even his (or your) fantasies as much as just desires and needs. Of course, that could be uncomfortable and maybe even risky for many women—maybe even some men. We are so conditioned to be afraid to share ourselves that deeply with another person for fear of rejection. But don't you think if we are married to someone we should be able to risk being *that* open and intimate with one another? Some people would find it easier to tell their deepest fantasies to a stranger than to their spouse. I find that sad. The one person in the whole world you should be able to trust with your heart—with your deepest desires—should be your spouse.

Having sex with the same person over the course of several decades can become mechanical if steps are not taken to keep things "spiced" up. I'm not saying it takes work, but it does take intentionality—by both partners. Part of keeping things fresh and alive is developing the sexual intimacy to enjoy each others' bodies and minds. To do that frequently requires a man to continuously cherish and honor his woman, and a wife to respect and admire her husband.

A woman should understand though that if she is not actively pursuing her husband sexually it may negate every other demonstration of her love. And men need to recognize that silence in response to a woman's need for communication can be just as devastating to their sex life.

Understanding and Fulfilling Her Sexual Needs

Any guy out there who doesn't want to have sex more often, raise your hand. That's what I thought—no takers. I'm of the opinion that sex is like brownies. They are all good, some are just better than others. Here are a few things to keep in mind to improve your sex life, guys.

Many females are wired to respond sexually to nonsexual affection. They like being romanced with gifts like flowers and cards, whisperings of "sweet nothings" in their ear, and rapt attention to them. They are stimulated by intense verbal interaction. They have a *need* to be pursued.

When women get that "need" for nonphysical affection fulfilled, they are programmed to respond with sexual affection. It's why guys who learn to speak the "language" that women respond to always score a lot. I knew a guy in the service who charged other men to teach them how to, for lack of a better word, "seduce" women. He taught young men how to speak a woman's language. And he seemed to be pretty effective. At least I don't remember anyone asking for refunds.

The female always gives herself to the male. Even our sexual apparatus suggests the male "plug-in" (or giving or inserting) and the female "receptacle" (or receiving). The lexicon of language supports this: she "gives herself away" or "he takes her." You've never heard a circumstance where a woman "took" a man sexually. Unless coerced, the decision is always hers to make whether or not to "give" herself to a man. When a man takes you on a date and pays for everything, he is essentially buying the pleasure of your company (but not your body).

Not in a prostitution-like way, but he's purchasing the right to see if you are interested in him—nothing more, nothing less. This "unwritten rule" or understanding allows women the control of the initial relationship to be able to protect herself from harmful, shallow, or dangerous encounters (or being seduced by a young man who went through a course to teach him how to speak her language). By giving that right away (by acting as sexually aggressive as a male), she opens herself up to being used and abandoned. Because women control the decision to have sex, what are some factors that she uses to make that decision? And what are some factors that women complain about regarding their husbands in this area?

Over the years I've heard many women complain about their husband's lack of sensitivity and thoughtfulness in this area of their marriage. And from some of the things I've heard, I don't blame them. The most frequent complaint I hear is that their husband only cares about satisfying his own needs. This often translates into a scenario something like this: (1) no or limited foreplay, (2) jumps on and does his business as quickly and efficiently as possible, and (3) rolls over and falls asleep as soon as he is done.

Hello? What's wrong with this picture? Could it be selfish and self-centered? Frankly, it's a little embarrassing to think that some of my brethren think it is acceptable to act this way. It would be like someone putting a bowl of ice cream in front of you and then hogging it all down before you could get a bite.

An important concept to keep in mind is that your wife's entire world is tied into her sex life. Now I know from experience that if a guy is struggling at work, he can put that area of his life in a box and still eagerly want and enjoy sex. In fact sex can often act as a soothing or healing agent for a man.

Unfortunately, though, women are not made to respond this way. So if the children are sick, if you've been arguing, if the house is a mess, if finances are tight, if you have scheduled a move, or any one of a thousand other daily factors of life, these play into her ability to desire and enjoy sex. And if she's lost respect for you or is angry at you, she is often physically unable to have sexual relations. That's generally just the opposite for men. Any of you guys out there have trouble having sex with your wife if you're peeved at her? I didn't think so. You might act all petulant about it, but given the right circumstances you'd be just as eager as always.

It's a myth that women do not enjoy sex as much as men. If a woman has not been abused or damaged emotionally, psychologically, or physically, God created her to enjoy sex just as much as a man. Like everything else in life, she just has different needs in this area. When a man figures out how to fulfill those needs, he suddenly finds that his wife is just as willing a participant as he is. One of the main needs she requires to be met is the need for romance.

Men—How Not to Get Your Needs Fulfilled

A three-year-old boy was examining his testicles while taking a bath.

"Mom," he asked, "are these my brains? "

"Not yet," she replied.

If sex is one of a man's primary needs (and it is), how can you get your needs met in this area? After all, due to lesser amounts of testosterone, your wife's sex drive is usually lower (or at least less urgent) than yours is and she isn't wired to need sexual release as often or in as many varieties of ways.

The question often comes up in my workshops for moms raising boys whether masturbation is normal and whether or not it is healthy for boys and men. From our hundreds of discussions, I suspect their real concern actually centers around the fact that many of these women have husbands or boyfriends who spend more than their share of time watching online pornography. Since it's virtually impossible to watch pornography and not masturbate, this leads to many of these women not getting the kind of physical affection they need. (Males at twenty-five years old might be able to masturbate three times a day and still make love at the drop of a hat. At forty-five they can't.) Or worse, being asked or forced to perform sexual acts that are uncomfortable or unnatural, but which are commonplace in pornography.

I've written quite a bit in my previous books about the topic of masturbation and its consequences for males, and so I don't want to rehash it all here. The question that generally comes up for Christians is whether or not masturbation is a sin. Certainly many pastors would say it is a sin, whereas most secular academics would claim it is a normal function of life.

Whether or not masturbation is morally or ethically wrong I can't say with any certainty. Like most issues it's seldom black and white, but colored with many shades of gray. (For instance, is it immoral for a man to engage in this act periodically if his wife is physically unable to perform for an extended period of time, and he only thinks about his wife when he does it? I suspect that scenario is less egregious than a man fantasizing about the sixteen-year-old cheerleader down the street.)

Here's what I can say with certainty—on some level masturbation is a betrayal of your wife. With that said, there's nothing in the Bible that directly forbids masturbation (although both the commandment about not coveting your neighbor's wife and Jesus's admonition not to lust after another woman probably relate at least indirectly to this topic). There's no 11th Commandment that states, "Thou shalt not take matters into thine own hands." It would make it a lot easier if there were, but God chose to be somewhat ambiguous about this subject for reasons known only to him.

Nevertheless, fantasizing about other women is not healthy for your relationship. Your wife will be deeply wounded and have a sense of betrayal as this attacks her at one of the core issues of her insecurity—her desirability. In addition, masturbation is a narcissistic action—it is self-pleasure with no regard for the feelings or needs of your wife.

Pornography is destroying more marriages than any other factor in recent years. Over half (56 percent) of all divorces involve one person who is involved with pornography.[4] It causes a man to get his physical satisfaction from other sources and decreases his desire for his wife. When his wife feels undesirable, she naturally gets either insecure or bitter and resentful. Neither scenario is good for your relationship.

Porn is dangerous because it's so incredibly addictive. The chemicals released in the brain when viewing it create a "high." Like any addicting substance or activity, it should be avoided if for no other reason than it creates escalating behavior and requires greater amounts in order to achieve the same "high." Most married men wouldn't think of dabbling with heroin, but maybe because it's legal we think we can play around with porn and not get burned.

Guys, you want to have better sex more often? The solution is simple. Stop looking at porn, romance your wife, and make her life easier any way you can.

Cleanliness Is Next to Sexiness

First of all, guys, let's admit that only women look good without their clothes on. No guy I've ever seen in the locker room looked good naked. In fact, men shouldn't even wear Lycra. Sorry, "bicycle guy," but your skinny, saggy behind does not look good ensconced in Lycra no matter how much you think you look like Lance Armstrong. And for you other guys, Lycra wasn't meant to stretch that much.

One of the items that quite a few of the women I surveyed for this book commented on was their husbands' personal hygiene habits (or lack thereof). Most women value cleanliness more than men do (at least they always smell better). While I'd like to give you guys the benefit of the doubt here, I think the ladies are talking about some basic sanitation functions.

Before I talk about some of these things that bother the women who responded to my survey, let me say that personally I don't care. You can be as uncouth and smelly as you want and it won't bother me. But if you want a more satisfying sex life, it might be important to listen to what the women had to say. Here's my spin on their feedback:

> *Body odor:* I like my manly armpit odor as much as the next guy, but come on, guys. Frankly, I don't blame the gals here. I wouldn't want to swap bodily fluids with someone who stinks either. It seems like it's just respect and common courtesy that if you want to get some sugar, you take a shower first—or at least sometime within the preceding twenty-four hours. It's just a myth that bathing more than once a month is unhealthy. I know some of you guys actually work for a living (as opposed to being a writer), but clean hands and fingernails are not less manly than dirty ones, and BO is not a badge of masculinity.

Change your clothes at least twice a week. I have my favorite lounging-around-the-house sweatpants too, but even I have to admit they get a little rank every so often. If you've been working on the car, she probably won't appreciate you sitting on the couch in your oil-stained jeans. In fairness though, I'll admit that the threadbare, hole-filled favorite T-shirt you've worn since college is off-limits and should *not* be thrown away by her, no matter how terrible it looks on you.

Also, *brush your teeth before you start kissing on her.* Not only is a clean mouth healthier, it's also sexier. I think I've talked to some of you guys these ladies are referring to and they have a point. If your breath makes the eyes of the person you are talking to water, it's time to brush. Green teeth are only cool in Star Trek movies and Charlie Daniels songs.

And *cut your toenails every once in awhile.* No one thinks those long yellow horny things are sexy except you. You older guys need to trim your nose and ear hair occasionally too. I don't care what you think, that's not a sophisticated look on anyone.

Frankly, the fairer sex puts up with a lot just sleeping with most of us beasts to begin with. Between the ubiquitous male qualities of back hair, belly fat, and unending flatulence, I'm surprised we ever get lucky at all.

The Other Side of the Story

Because men were created as visual beings, a woman's physical appearance is the first thing that a man notices. Many women feel this is shallow, but it makes sense from a biological perspective. God seemed to know what he was doing when he created men and women. He biologically created males to be very visual and filled with testosterone, which ensured the male would pursue the female with the urge to procreate. He then designed these very visual, hormone-driven beings to be at their sexual peak in their late teens, about the same time that the female of the species is at the height of her physical attractiveness. This ensured that the male, to fulfill his sexual needs, would stay with his mate until such time as he matured and the testosterone levels dropped enough that he was more capable of developing a mature, loving relationship. While sex is still important to him, his sexual appetite begins to ebb just about the time the female reaches her sexual peak, just in time to reinvigorate his sexual capacity and extend the relationship.

Of course the first thing that attracted him to you was your looks—you know that. It's ridiculous to pretend otherwise or to be offended by it. It's how he was created—how he is biologically designed. Illogically, some women get offended when a man admires her for her looks, yet they frequently use it to their advantage whenever necessary. (I notice women who work in the little drive-up coffee kiosks here in the Pacific Northwest usually wear low-cut tops or even bikinis. That way when they bend over to hand a man his coffee, they end up getting bigger tips.) My wife and daughter get great deals when we go to traditionally masculine events like gun shows or car shows, deals that I would never get offered. Guys working the booths practically throw free stuff at them. The power of sexual attraction is a valuable commodity in the marketplace when understood and used advantageously. Of course I'm probably promoting sexual stereotypes about men—and women—again.

A man's perception of a woman's physical attractiveness may even allow him to overlook irritating habits or aspects of a woman's personality as well. Especially in the earlier years of a relationship, he may stay with her through times when he does not "like" her because he still lusts for her. This "staying" then allows him to develop his love for her deep enough to eventually weather the relational traumas that happen in every marriage.

Whether they'll admit it or not, most women are flattered by attention to their physical appearance. But you can't have it both ways, ladies. Either you enjoy getting looked at because you are a female or you don't. But don't dress provocatively, then complain about what pigs men are.

Every day I see women who dress in tight, low-cut tops, short skirts, form-fitting yoga pants, or short shorts. Then they get indignant because men are looking at them. Please. You know men are visual. If you don't want their attention, then don't show off the goods. If you show it, we'll look at it. Do some men go too far with the leering and ogling? Of course they do and they need to be reprimanded. But I heard a young woman go on a diatribe about what pigs men were because they were looking at her and honking at her during her bike ride. When I asked what she was wearing, it amounted to less than a total of a couple of hand spans of material. Give me a break! She's lucky she didn't cause an accident.

How to Have Great Sex for a Lifetime

Respect is a big part of marriage. A woman needs to make sure she finds a man to marry whom she respects, not just loves. Not only is it imperative that a man be respected by the woman he loves, but it is crucial for the woman to respect him for the marriage to survive. When a woman loses respect for a man, it signals the beginning of the loss of love for him.

Marriage is a relationship of cycles or seasons. There will be times (seasons) when a woman will not like her man very much. In fact, there will probably be times when she might dislike him strongly to one degree or another. If she respects him, she will weather those storms and stay the course. If she does not respect him, she will be more likely to leave him or end the marriage.

This brings up another interesting point, guys. Your wife chose you out of all the men in the world. She chose *you* to spend her entire life with. She chose you as the man she wanted to have children with, to grow old together with. She chose to align herself with you by association. Since relationships are integral in determining a woman's self-image, her choice of a man reflects heavily upon her personage. Your character reflects upon her in so many ways. Other women judge her by the quality of the man she attracted, just like men judge you by the beauty of the woman you "captured." Neither scenario is discussed openly, but you know in your heart this is true.

After she read an email from a soldier whose life had been profoundly impacted by one of my books, a young woman sent my wife this comment: "What a great life Rick has come to live! Emails like these must just truly make you so proud to be his wife."

My actions reflect upon my wife. They can reflect upon her positively or negatively. It's my choice, but the truth is, the way I live life is not just about me. My wife and children are impacted by it as well.

That all being true, perhaps if a man worked on his character in order to be the kind of man his wife was proud to be associated with—one she respected and admired—perhaps she would be more eager to have sex with him. That kind of man would make her look better to her peers and feel better about herself because of the quality of mate she attracted. Those factors can generate feelings of intimacy in a woman, which is known to lead to physical desire. It builds her self-esteem, which leads to feeling good about herself. Women who feel good about themselves are always more interested in having sex. I can't prove this theory is true scientifically, but it does seem logical. Test it out and see if it's true for you.

Intimacy-Building Tips for More Sexuality with Your Spouse

- Women—make sure your husband knows you are attracted to him and "want" him. Men—make sure your wife feels loved, cherished, and appreciated throughout the day, every day. Remember her whole life connects. You can't upset her at breakfast, then expect to get frisky that night.
- Ladies—be aware of your physical appearance. Men—be aware of your character and strive to make sure your wife respects and admires you.
- Share your physical needs and desires with your spouse. This may be more difficult for some wives, but, ladies, remember men can't read your mind. They need to be told exactly what you need and how you need it in all areas of life, including the bedroom. Sometimes experimentation with role playing or other fun games can help get these needs met in a nonthreatening manner.

6

Our Woundedness

Turning Mud into Bricks

The woundings from our past, sometimes
inflicted generations ago, cripple our ability
to love today, and the only empire we can
build is one of insecurity, distrust, and self-
loathing. Unfortunately that's what we are
now seeing in our families and in so many
facets of our society.

—Warwick Marsh

The wounds that we receive to our heart and soul can
either cripple us or motivate us to accomplish great
things in life. Undoubtedly they are one of the biggest
obstacles to having more intimacy in our relationship. Our
wounds determine the way we respond to things that are said

to us and how we treat others in our life. Wounds that are not dealt with sit and fester within us until they eventually spew their venom onto those we love and care about. But wounds that are healed can become a source of great inspiration and wisdom. We all have wounds in our heart. When two people try to meld together to become one in marriage, those wounds are a major stumbling block to having an intimate, loving relationship. The old saying that "you can't love someone else until you love yourself" rings with truth. When we are focused on our own emotional pain, we can't identify the real issues in our marriage. Focusing on our own needs prevents us from having the reserves to help deal with our spouse's needs. The truth is, your spouse is not responsible for your pain (unless he or she caused it), but you *are* responsible for how you respond to that pain. When I speak to men, I frequently tell them that if their father abandoned them, they have a right to be angry. But they do not have a right to pass that anger on to their wives and children.

I was recently listening to a talk by neuropsychologist Dr. Mario Martinez who said that all wounds can be narrowed down to three categories: shame (which feels hot in the body), abandonment (feels cold), and betrayal (hot/anger). Shame, he said, is healed by experiencing honoring. Abandonment is healed by experiencing commitment. And betrayal is healed by experiencing loyalty. If that's true, understanding our spouse's wounds can tell us how to help them heal those wounds or at least to more effectively deal with them.

My wife was abandoned by both her father (whom she only met briefly twice) and by her mother who quit parenting her at ten years old (she subsequently left home at age thirteen). Hence she had great abandonment issues when we got married. She didn't trust that I wouldn't abandon her and she jealously guarded her heart. Being abandoned again was her greatest fear. She even had a tendency to try to push me to the point where I would leave (probably an unconscious attempt to test my level of commitment). It has taken the better part of three decades of modeling commitment on my part for her to finally start trusting that I will not abandon her. My level of commitment has at best healed and at worst scarred over the jagged wound of abandonment in her heart.

Not all wounds are that difficult to address. But it's understandable to see how a person who feels ashamed about themselves could find healing by being honored by the one who loves them. So, men, if your wife is ashamed of her body and how she looks, you telling her (and showing her) how beautiful she is can go a long way to making her feel better about herself. Ladies, if your husband is ashamed by his past failures, your belief in him is honoring and can heal those wounds as well.

Likewise, someone who has been betrayed can only be made to feel better about themselves by experiencing loyalty. When we know the person we love cares for us enough to stand by us, defending us behind our back—even to the important people in their life (such as their parents)—then the sting of past betrayal begins to fade.

As a caveat it's important to understand that professional counseling is an integral part of healing from any psychological and emotional wounds we might suffer from. In addition, if you are a Christian, you understand that God is truly the Great Physician, and his touch of unconditional love, grace, and forgiveness heals even the most egregious wounds. Let's begin.

Our Baggage

> The greatest gift you can give to somebody is your own personal development. I used to say, "If you will take care of me, I will take care of you." Now I say, "I will take care of me for you, if you will take care of you for me."
>
> —Jim Rohn

All people come into a marriage with baggage caused by a variety of sources—childhood wounds, parental modeling, and social conditioning are just a few. Some people have been raised relatively healthy and have only a small amount of baggage, and some of us have so much baggage we can barely walk through the door, but everyone has some.

Marriage is a "people growing" process. The sacrifices that marriage requires prepare us for the challenges of child-raising and develop us as "whole" human beings. Nobody is ever ready or prepared for marriage—marriage *is* what makes us ready for marriage. Oftentimes our baggage causes problems as our marriage progresses and we find ourselves in stressful situations (which *always* occur in marriages). In fact, times of stress often bring wounds we have suppressed to the surface. Because we don't like discomfort, we then immediately look for an easy cure or fix for the problem.

But all problems aren't meant to be fixed—at least not easily. Many deep wounds take years of painful examination and insight to get a handle on. In addition, suffering generally helps create character. The challenges you've been through have developed a part of who you are—often the best parts. Lastly, God tends to use our worst wounds (if we are willing) to minister through us to others.

Wounded people are often used to living lives of chaos. Living in chaos creates stress and causes our bodies to respond with higher levels of hormones like cortisol, adrenaline, norepinephrine. If we live under those conditions long enough, our bodies eventually become comfortable at those levels and it actually becomes uncomfortable to live without stress. Have you ever noticed when you place people from very stressful homes in a calm, healthy environment, they will create some sort of chaos? When you are used to living in crisis mode, it is understandable that you would be uncomfortable in a peaceful environment. The problem is that people then bring these behaviors and crises into their marriage.

Life and marriage, with their self-made crises, don't often get smoothed over easily. Typically the emotional knots and gridlocks we create require painstaking work in order to untangle. Most couples think that they shouldn't be having so many problems—that if they were really in love, marriage wouldn't be so hard. They also tend to think other couples do not have the same problems as they do. This causes them to feel inadequate, angry, and resentful. But the truth is, all couples suffer from the same issues to one degree or another. It is the way we perceive those problems and then deal with them that determines whether we have a loving marriage or one that is filled with strife and bitterness. Usually people's fantasies and unrealistic expectations regarding marriage are the biggest problems in their relationship. Here's the truth—marriage is hard! It's never been easy. All throughout history average men and women have struggled with their marriages.

We all tend to suffer with the same problems; some couples have just learned effective strategies for dealing with their issues.

We have a misconception that relationships are supposed to be easy—that we should never have problems. And if we do, it's suddenly "not meant to be." Human beings tend to avoid conflict. We don't discuss important issues—we scream that the person who disagrees with us is a "hater." A small tiff causes us to leave the room (or un-friend someone), and friction causes us to be uncomfortable at best and become bitter and zone out at worst. We don't want to endure the struggle of fixing the problem, so we either ignore it or leave it. If your marriage is broken, fix it! Don't throw it away. We live in a disposable culture. If we get tired of something or it is slightly used, it's easier to dispose of it rather than take good care of it and keep it in working order. If you are serious about your marriage being a lifelong relationship, you have to spend time doing maintenance on it. You have to do things that prevent it from breaking or wearing out. You wouldn't spend tens of thousands of dollars to buy a car and then never put oil or coolant into it. Instead you perform preventative maintenance like changing the oil, brakes, and tires when they get old. You occasionally change the air and oil filters so that dirt doesn't get into the insides and grind down the parts. If you don't do that kind of maintenance, the friction between the moving parts will not be smooth and eventually they'll either overheat and warp or become scored and ragged. The same thing happens in relationships when we don't purposefully spend the time and effort in making sure they run smoothly. Certainly your marriage and family relationships are more important and valuable than a car.

If you are struggling, I encourage you to seek professional counseling sooner than later. Most people wait to get help until it's almost too late. Counseling helps you learn about yourself and what prompts each of you to act the way you do and make the decisions and choices that you each do. That in itself is worth the cost and work required to take advantage of counseling services.

If you have a short-term vision of marriage, you won't spend any effort or energy trying to make it work. You won't read books, attend seminars, or get personal and couples counseling. In short, the length of your vision directly corresponds with the length of time you'll probably be married.

How Our Backgrounds Affect Us

A woman came up to me after I had spoken at a conference and said, "I loved your talk and speaking style. You remind me of an educated workingman." I must admit I didn't really know whether that was a compliment or a criticism. After reflection, I realized she had that impression because that's exactly what I am. I was raised in a lower middle class, blue-collar neighborhood. Both my parents were straight off the farm from Wisconsin. Despite the fact that I have a graduate degree I have a working-class pedigree.

That comment got me to thinking about how we are raised and how much we are actually able to change from our early childhood programming. For instance, I have well exceeded the socioeconomic status of my upbringing—I am college educated, have started several successful businesses, am a published author, and interface successfully with people from all walks of life. Yet something about me (within me) told that woman what my background was and—in essence—*who* I was. Our roots develop within us a character or personification that no matter how much we might try to change, our heritage remains. It shows in our mien, our demeanor, our attitude, how we carry ourselves, even how we talk and walk. It shows up in our language and communication style—our accents, our inflections, our emphasis on certain words and the colloquialisms we use. It shows in the clothes we wear, how we wear them, our style or élan, and our belief or attitude of where we belong in the world.

Psychologically it shows in how we feel about ourselves (our self-esteem) and how we see ourselves (our self-image). Despite the fact I have had years of counseling, training, education, and intentional growth, I still have some essence of blue-collar workingman in me. I joked with my wife that there should be "finishing schools" for people like me to polish off the rough edges of my working-class heritage.

You'll notice that people can always pick out those who are not from their background (it's pretty easy to tell the difference between someone raised in an affluent area of Boston versus someone from a poor neighborhood in Birmingham, Alabama). The poor kid who gets a scholarship to Harvard or Princeton is glaringly out of place and never quite fits in. Even the middle-class kid who goes to a poor neighborhood stands out like a sore thumb. Try as we might to bury it, our past hovers over us like the shadows in a graveyard. Oftentimes it doesn't matter how we dress or how much education we have. Even wearing an expensive suit and watch with Italian loafers, I probably would not be as comfortable in a big corporate boardroom environment as someone who grew up with that expectation and training. My demeanor, attitude, and language would give me away (although I've learned one way to make people think I'm smarter than I am is to just keep my mouth shut).

My wife comes from a hardscrabble home life as well. Even in a designer gown with diamond earrings she might have a difficult time fitting in at a highbrow social function merely because she does not know the language, the habits, the customs, and the nuances of social protocol of people from that pedigree nor the confidence that comes with it (although my wife is a lot classier than I am and might be able to pull it off). My point is, even though she is just as intelligent and elegant as women from that background, she'll probably never be confused for someone who has had debutante training and attended a finishing school before going off to Bryn Mawr, Radcliffe, or Vassar College.

Childhood Wounds

Everyone also has some wounds from childhood. Some are slight and barely noticeable; others are monsters that ravage a person's soul.

Childhood wounds encompass a wide variety of abuses in any number of areas including sexual assault, molestation, or exploitation; physical abuse; emotional (and psychological) abuse; abandonment; or neglect. In data from 2011, approximately 676,000 children were reported to have suffered from some sort of abuse. Of those, 75 percent involved neglect, 15 percent physical abuse, and 10 percent suffered from sexual abuse.[1] Of course, a lot of abuse (especially sexual) is never reported or discovered, so it's safe to assume that a much greater number of people have been abused than are reported. Few families escape having at least one member being sexually abused.

Often those who abuse children were themselves abused as children. As the "survivor" of an alcoholic home, I can tell you that abuse comes in all forms and formats. Hollywood likes to portray alcoholics as tragically romantic figures, like in the movies *Under the Volcano*, *Leaving Las Vegas*, and *The Last Samurai*. In reality, most drunks are damaged and broken figures. They crush other people's souls and spew battery acid on the hearts of the innocent victims who love them, rendering those around them wounded and in pain. Mental health experts consider alcoholism a "disease." I consider a disease to be something you can't control whether or not you will get, like multiple sclerosis. I consider alcoholism to be a bad choice. People may have a predisposition to getting it, but in the end it is still a conscious choice each individual makes.

Abuse can also come in the form of abandonment. Because of the work I have done in this area, I can generally tell pretty quickly when I meet someone who either had no father or an abusive father. There are certain telltale signs from someone who has extensive "father wounds." Likewise, certain behaviors signal to a professionally trained person that someone has been sexually abused as a child. Even the way a person carries themselves (their body language) gives cues as to their potential childhood wounds.

Those wounds often haunt us throughout our lives, keeping us from being the kind of person we were created to be. Getting help for these kinds of wounds is difficult. But the truth is, it will never be easier to get help than it will be right now. The longer the wounds fester, the more difficult it becomes to address them.

When we are wounded (especially in childhood), we tend to create "self-talk" related to that wound. For instance, if you've been abused, you might feel unworthy or that you somehow deserved to be abused. Additionally, words spoken to us by our care providers tend to embed themselves in our hearts. If a father or mother tells us we are "no good" or "stupid," we tend to subconsciously believe that. Our unconscious mind then creates "tapes" that play those words over and over again even when we don't recognize it's happening. This phenomenon causes us to self-sabotage ourselves throughout life as those old tapes roll over and over again, telling us what we cannot accomplish and why. Those tapes are almost never true.

Women in general seem to have a lot of internal dialogue that goes on inside their head. Much of this is self-critical and feeds their anxiety and feelings of worthlessness or inadequacy. Wounded women in particular tend to have a lot of insecurities—their self-esteem and self-image suffer.

So stop those negative mental tapes that keep telling you things about yourself that are just not true. Those voices are usually words spoken to us as children by people who were themselves wounded individuals. We tend to give those voices more credence than the positive words of affirmation from those who love us and only want the best for us. You deserve better—and so does your family.

Past Relationship Wounds

Most people are prone to bring past relationship wounds into their current relationships. These wounds are particularly destructive because your current partner has no idea what you are talking about or where you are coming from. So for instance, if your spouse was cheated on in the past, he/she will often distrust a future spouse. Conversely, the wounded person needs to pause and remember that the person he or she is currently with did not perform the act (or say the words) that created the wound. Much like our criminal justice system, that person should be considered innocent until proven guilty—they should be given the benefit of the doubt. Likewise when a person has been wounded by a mother or father while growing up, it is difficult not to reflect that behavior in future relationships. In these circumstances trust and truthfulness are important factors in helping your spouse understand your wounds and how best to deal with them.

If you've ever experienced abuse or dysfunction in the past, you know fear makes you believe that the next relationship may be worse, that you may be hurt more and loved less. Those are false voices based on your wounds and the evil ones who wish to see you tortured. Fear and distrust are the enemies of intimacy in a relationship. Shine light on those fears by sharing them and they become less destructive.

People who have past relationship wounds are often dependent on their partner for their happiness. They receive validation and contentment by how their spouse treats them or the attitude their spouse displays. This dependency makes it very difficult for either spouse to maintain a healthy attitude.

But partners who do not depend on their spouse for validation can remain intimate even during times of stress and conflict. They use each other's strengths to fuel their relationship instead of allowing their weaknesses to destroy it. When we allow another person to validate our worth, we give them the control to manipulate our lives.

Unfortunately, the more emotionally unhealthy a person is, the more apt they are to engage in highly dependent relationships. Because these people don't handle anxiety well (they aren't able to comfort themselves), every time their partner becomes upset, they do as well. And since they are dependent upon their partner for reinforcement, they then spend vast amounts of energy trying to control their partner and the relationship in order to get control of themselves. A lot of emotional energy is expended in a generally frustrating and often fruitless cause. In the alcoholic home where I grew up, whenever my mother got upset, everyone paid for it. So we each either left the house or spent much of our time and energy trying to make sure she was happy, contented, and anxiety free. But it was a no-win battle. She continued to negatively control and manipulate things regardless of what herculean efforts we performed.

At some point a person gets tired of this game and either individually grows and learns to validate him or herself, or leaves the situation—often repeating it in another scenario (like a second marriage). It's one of the reasons why second marriages have an even higher failure rate than first marriages.

A Woman's Wounds

Last summer I paid a professional photographer to do a photo shoot of both my wife and daughter. I wanted my daughter to have some mementos of herself at age twenty-four at the peak of her physical beauty, and I wanted my wife to have professional photos of her great beauty before she got old enough that her physical appearance started to change.

(Note—my wife insisted that I add that she never thought of herself as beautiful; more a sultry, attractive redhead.) And I thought it would be fun to have some photos of them together as adults.

It was an interesting experience and one from which I learned a valuable lesson. The photographer was obviously stunned by my daughter's youthful beauty. He spent much time with her, often gushing about how great she looked. My wife, relegated to the sidelines, quickly developed a rather sour attitude about the whole affair and did not enjoy the experience, even when she was being photographed. I have come to understand that for her entire life, my wife was used to being the center of attention due to her beauty (even if she never felt beautiful). I think she was shocked (and probably surprised) to find herself disappointed at playing "second fiddle" to her own daughter. While I don't think it would be fair to say she was jealous, I do think that she was a little dismayed, and deep in her heart saddened, to be in that unexpected position, possibly for the first time in her life. (Because of her wounds, what she failed to realize was her true beauty was internal and showed through in the photographs that he had taken of her.) Anyone viewing those photos would think she was beautiful both inside and out. Her past wounds caused her to regard the situation she was in from a warped perspective, creating unnecessary pain.

Due to various factors—fatherlessness, abuse, pain, abandonment, bullying, and any number of other hurts—women have bought into the lies that their worth is based on how they look or on their sexuality. They attempt to be strong in order to avoid trusting a man and risk being hurt by someone again. They feel something is wrong if they are not achieving things that our culture considers significant. They believe that if only their circumstances or job or situation were different, "I would be okay and loved." In the midst of all this, they've forgotten or never learned how to be a little girl just being loved in a daddy's arms. These wounds then tend to unconsciously affect their decision-making process, leading them to places in life they never thought they would end up. The devastation is not only in molestation or abandonment, but in the wasted and often toxic lives that follow. My mother was deeply scarred in childhood and never took any steps to heal from her wounds. Instead, she self-medicated with alcohol her entire adult life. Her not healing from her childhood wounds deeply impacted my life and my siblings' lives as well.

Daughters especially are crushed by their woundedness (remember, men, each of you are married to somebody's daughter). They become women who carry those wounds around in their hearts for the rest of their lives.

So many women never understand their value. I've spent a lifetime with a woman who, because she was damaged as a child, has never fully appreciated her value and beauty as a woman (maybe even as a human being). Despite my attempts (which at times felt heroic to me) to encourage and help heal her heart, she still does not fully believe she is beautiful. This rip in her heart can only be healed by God. My mortal attempts are easily batted away by whispers from the Master of Lies who planted his seeds in her subconscious when evil was being perpetrated upon her as a child by bad men.

Our culture gives a lot of lip service to wanting to empower our young women in healthier ways than just through their physical appearance, and yet the messages sent (and reinforced) by women themselves are that their looks matter more to them than they do to men. Females judge each other very harshly regarding their looks all the time. Women buy most of the magazines that are destructive to girls' and women's self-esteem and psyches.

Paradoxically, women seem to be much harder on other women (and themselves) than they are on men. You would think women would understand the obstacles other women face in this area and would be more compassionate with one another. But it seems more often a case of "if I can make you feel bad about yourself, I'll feel better about myself." For all the talk about how women are relational, it's the men who are, in reality, probably more so. Put three men who don't know each other in a room together and chances are good within five minutes they've found a problem to fix together. Put three women in a room together and within five minutes two of them will hate the third, and if one leaves the room, the other two will talk about her behind her back.

That's an overdramatized stereotype but might well have a seed of truth nonetheless. Men—despite being biologically designed to be more aggressive—tend to generally get along pretty well with each other. Women, for all their nurturing tendencies, seem to be really hard on one another. My wife just came back from the doctor's office and used the following words to describe the women working in the reception area—backbiting, snide, and critical of each other. I see posts and blogs all the time where women (Christian women too) viciously attack celebrities or other women for an ounce of cellulite on their thighs or for the clothes they wear, their makeup, or their hairstyles. And it goes on and on.

A Man's Wounds

Wounded hearts are not exclusive to women. A man may bury his wounds much deeper, because analyzing hurts and expressing feelings generally doesn't come as easily. Some of those wounds include being disrespected (especially by his wife), the failures he experiences in life, and not attaining the success he envisions for himself. The resulting feelings of inadequacy or incompetence wound men deeply. Boys who get picked last for the team are wounded just as much as men who don't get the promotion at work. A man who cannot make his wife happy or has one who is perpetually discontented feels inadequate and suffers the sting of that failure. A man who continually fails feels defeated and worthless.

These wounds strike at the heart of his masculinity, causing him to question his worth and value as a man. That's the question a man frequently, yet secretly asks himself: "Do I have what it takes? Am I a real man?" A man who fails at work *and* at home can only assume that he does *not* have what it takes. Give him success in one area or the other and he can live with it, but take away both and he might be inclined to leave that life for one that offers hope or settle for being a shell of a man. A man will stay with something he is successful at because he gets good feelings from it. So if a man struggles at home but is successful at work, what's his motivation to spend more time at home?

Healing Our Past Wounds—Together

> Transformation without work and pain, without suffering, without a sense of loss is just an illusion of true change.
>
> —William Paul Young, *Cross Roads*

The truth is, you can never change your spouse, you can only change yourself. Your spouse may choose to change in response to the changes they observe in you. When that happens, you begin to grow together as a couple and wondrous things happen. But positive change and growth are painful and difficult. It's precisely why more people don't change and grow. Change takes time and effort—usually a long time. Permanent change is generally not a short-term endeavor.

It's been my experience that broken people tend to take advice from other broken people, instead of from healthy people who could give them advice that would help. They do this because other broken people tell them the things they want to hear. Of course following that advice is guaranteed to keep them in the same cycle of dysfunction they've lived in their entire lives. Since broken people generally marry other broken people, it often takes outside sources such as counselors, mentors, or healthy friends and family to help couples grow together. Be aware as you begin the process that growing together out of brokenness takes enormous reserves of patience, courage, and perseverance from both spouses. But trust me, it's worth the effort.

One of the nice things about marriage is that it is a natural conduit to begin the healing process. Some psychologists refer to the "polishing" process of marriage as *differentiation*. Differentiation balances individuality and togetherness. Differentiation is the process by which each spouse maintains a healthy self-identity while developing an intimate, loving, bonding relationship with another. It is the ability to maintain your sense of self even when emotionally close to others. It helps prevent our wounds and baggage from interfering with the attainment of deeper intimacy and more passionate sex with our spouse. But it also keeps us from becoming enmeshed in trying to fulfill our spouse's needs at the sake of our own well-being. Differentiation develops tenderness, generosity, and compassion in a relationship. It enables the person to keep from holding grudges and to recover quickly from arguments, while still maintaining one's individual needs and priorities. Differentiation is a lifelong process that shapes and grows an individual and a couple to maintain their uniqueness and still cleave together as one.[2]

Psychologist and author David Schnarch says this about differentiation:

> Well-differentiated people can agree without feeling like they are "losing themselves," and can disagree without feeling alienated and embittered. They can stay connected with people who disagree with them and still "know who they are." They don't have to leave the situation to hold onto their sense of self.[3]

An important thing to remember about differentiation is that we tend to develop our level of differentiation in our teens and leave our parents' home at about the level of differentiation that they achieved. This level generally gets passed from one generation of a family to the next. Dysfunctional parents tend to pressure their children to behave the same way they do as a form of validating or regulating their own emotions. This keeps children from developing the ability to think, feel, and act for themselves.[4] I grew up in an alcoholic home where there were very strict rules regarding loyalty to the family (don't tell an outsider), autonomy (don't think you are better than each other by growing or challenging the status quo), and most importantly parenting (the adults' needs were most important so the children had to parent the parents). This certainly challenged my ability to expand my vision of the world and placed restrictions on how I was able to grow as an individual and together with my wife as a couple.

The second issue regarding our level of differentiation we need to understand is that it is hard to change. We also tend to marry someone who is at the same level as we are. While we like to *think* one spouse is much more advanced emotionally than the other, this is just not true. This factor requires both couples to change together in this area in order to effectively achieve results. Suzanne and I know from experience that as difficult as it is for one person to change their core beliefs and behavior patterns, it's even more difficult to get two people to work together on changing themselves as a team. But that's exactly what is necessary to grow and develop the intimacy required for a lifelong marriage. I advise men and women (especially if they are struggling) to go to not only couples counseling but also individual counseling. Yes, it's a challenging (and expensive) commitment, but a healthy relationship requires us to recognize what drives or causes us to act and think the way we do, and then to work together to understand how that challenges our relationship with our spouse.

One of the challenges that many couples face is that as human beings we are constantly growing and changing (although not always in a healthy direction). That means that eventually the person we are married to is not the same person we married. That can be a really good thing in some situations or very bad depending upon the direction that your spouse grows and changes. However if we do not grow together in certain directions, we end up growing apart. So, for instance, a person whose identity is dependent upon their relationship loses their identity when their spouse changes. Changes are very frightening to this person and they will often fight to keep even the most minor changes from happening. This can be very frustrating to their spouse, who interprets this behavior as stifling or controlling and generally rebels against it.[5]

Another challenge for marriages is that our Western civilization has become a very feelings-based culture. The problem with this is that not only do feelings change but they are not always true—they are perceptions based on a variety of experiences and interpretations, often beyond our control. In addition, feelings can change drastically from one moment to the next. They can even be manipulated (as can we) quite easily by someone who is knowledgeable in this area (advertising companies and politicians do it all the time).

Oftentimes people believe they *are* their feelings (someone who is considered "hotheaded" reacts with anger in all situations—that's who they *are*). But when we get our identity from our feelings, it creates other problems. We can't afford to have our feelings change or we'll feel like we don't know who we are.[6] Oftentimes in that situation when the partner grows or changes, it poses a threat to the person who identifies too closely or who "gets their identity" from that spouse. The dependent spouse resists the changes and is threatened by them.

As your partner becomes more important to you, you in turn become more vulnerable to losing their acceptance or even losing them altogether. This causes people to close off a part of themselves as a protective measure. Unfortunately, when we do that, it keeps us from having a deep, full relationship with our spouse, as they only know a part of us. It's difficult to be intimately involved with someone you don't know very well. It's why our wounds keep us from being as intimate and close to our spouses as we yearn to be.

Healing from wounds takes intentional effort and hard work. Suzanne and I spent years in couples and individual counseling (primarily due to the dysfunctional and abusive home lives we were both raised in). I can remember at various times during this process thinking things like, "There's been too much water under the bridge for this to work out" or "Is anything ever going to change? "Slowly but surely, over a long period of time, things got better. I woke up one day and, hey, things *were* better! But that journey required the ability to take a hard look at ourselves and the desire to change even when it hurt (and change always hurts). Besides counseling, we attended marriage conferences and workshops on a variety of relationship and healing programs, and read books together that were specific to our issues. Additionally we both attended groups individually. Because of my home background, I attended a group of Adult Children of Alcoholics (ACOA). Suzanne joined groups of women to help each other with issues like abandonment and abuse. We both feel we have at least graduate level college degrees in marriage relationships and pain management just because of all the work we went through.

If you've been seriously wounded in life, take steps to heal. It's virtually impossible to get the kind of intimacy you want with another person when you have wounds getting in the way. Serious dedication and hard work to heal some of those wounds works wonders. It's not easy—but it's worth it!

Intimacy-Building Tips to Turn Wounds into Benefits

- Work on your own issues, not your spouse's. You can't change them, only yourself. But oftentimes by changing yourself, others change around us in response to the changes they see.
- That said, understanding the wounds your spouse has goes a long way toward being a support as they work on their own issues.
- Understanding and recognizing (educating yourself on) your issues not only helps you to understand what motivates the choices and decisions you make but also keeps you from taking them out on your spouse or passing them down to your children. Ignorance is not bliss—it's destructive.
- If at all possible, try to grow together as a couple. Yes, each of us grows at our own pace, but going through these challenges together can bond you closer.

7

His Needs (for Her)

A frightened man has no loyalty to anyone—except the person he's most afraid of
at the moment.

—David Schnarch

What does a man need? Most men (at least from my generation) were taught not to talk about—and certainly not to complain about—their needs (except when we are sick, of course, then all bets are off). If I had to guess, I'd say that beyond a few obvious things, the majority of men don't even know what their needs are. While they might recognize when they are hungry, tired, or in need of sexual release, I doubt many men are introspective enough to understand how their emotional and psychological needs motivate their actions and decision-making process. And truthfully, even though I've been educated in this area, I still find myself reacting to various needs and not even realizing what is actually motivating me (if I'm hungry, all my psychological knowledge goes out the window). By not being in touch with my needs and understanding how they cause me to respond, I run the risk of not getting those needs met, as well as hurting others who care about me.

For instance, most men understand when something is physically wrong with them, yet many choose to ignore it rather than go to a doctor. They often do the same with their emotional challenges, choosing to ignore them rather than suffer the indignity of bringing them into the open and examining them. Is this a sign of weakness that men want to avoid admitting, even to themselves, they have weaknesses? Or would admitting these weaknesses somehow validate their existence? In other words, if a man ignores his weaknesses (which are actually needs rather than weaknesses), he can pretend they don't exist and maintain his persona of being invincible.

This chapter addresses just a few things that men need (besides sex) as they go through the different stages of life. It's not a comprehensive list at all of a male's needs, just a look at some topics that are not covered elsewhere in this book. These may give you some insight into what motivates your husband when his actions are confusing or do not seem to make sense. Remember, all people have a reason for everything they do, no matter how illogical or crazy it seems. Sometimes even we ourselves just don't know what these reasons are.

Men without Dads

The world is a frightening place. Life is hard. But it's even harder if you don't know how to live it properly. For men and boys who have not had mentoring or training in how a man should think, act, and solve problems or what his roles are in life, the struggle is even greater. As men, what we fear most of all is to appear incompetent or inadequate or to fail publicly. We run that risk every day when we don't know how to "do" life. That frightens us, often causing us to avoid anything that we might fail at. And when males are frightened, it can feel humiliating to them. So they typically cover it with another, less threatening emotion which they are more comfortable with—anger. There are a lot of angry young men out there. But they are not really angry, they are frightened. They are frightened because no one ever told them (or showed them) how a man, a husband, or a father lives his life and what his roles are. That frightens them, but it's not manly to be frightened, so they cover it with a more comfortable emotion or they avoid it all together. When you don't know what your roles are in life, it's pretty difficult to live up to them.

A significant portion of young men in the last generation have been raised without a father. Without that male role model, these men are at the mercy of having had only female role models and authority figures in their life or distant male role models from the media who are generally poor examples of masculinity.

And so, many men today are needy, unreliable little boys who seek approval from strangers because they don't approve of themselves. They never had the blessing of a father's teaching and the gift of his approval, which propels a male into life with confidence and self-esteem. Men with such low regard of themselves never respect others, especially those who love them. So we see young men who allow well-intentioned but misguided mothers to helicopter parent them into their thirties, eventually bankrupting these women financially and emotionally. We see a man who marries a woman and allows her to spend her life savings to pay off his debt and then expects her to work to support him while he engages in video games and drinks beers with his buddies. We find a plethora of young males who expect a woman to rescue them every time they get into trouble, because that's what they experienced growing up with just female role models. Many daughters tell me their mothers were much harder on them than on their brothers. They claim their brothers got away with things the mothers would never have have allowed the girls to get away with. The moms had much higher expectations for their daughters than they did their sons.

These men live life with a moral ambiguity that uses women and expects to be taken care of. They seldom live up to their masculine calling to provide for and protect those who might otherwise depend upon them. They are afraid to fail and they avoid anything that may be unpleasant, even if it's the very thing that is good for them. They frequently become skilled at quitting easily and fail to develop the intestinal fortitude required to succeed in life.

Needs of Younger Men

Healthy young men have a need to make their mark in the world. They yearn to find a battle to fight or a cause to champion—they crave significance. The bane for most men is that they never find a suitable challenge to which they can dedicate their lives.

Before marriage, most young men choose to act somewhat irresponsibly and engage in dangerous activities. Most of the dangerous and outrageous things young men do are geared toward accomplishing one thing—finding a female to mate with. Though they may not even be aware of what is motivating their actions, it's how males are biologically wired.

After marriage, most turn that energy into providing for their family and competing in the workplace as a way of landing in the pecking order of manhood. I know, a lot of readers will lament that masculinity is not determined by your job or accomplishments or how much money you make, and I agree. However, it's important to understand that most men garner at least some portion of their identity and self-esteem from what they do for a living and how successful they are at doing it.

Many young men believe a myth out there that says nice guys finish last, that women aren't interested in nice guys—they just use them or want them as "friends." But here's the deal, guys—a significant portion of women may indeed choose "bad boys" to have unfettered sex with in early adulthood (we'd like to say that good Christian girls don't, but statistics refute that). But nearly every woman—when she matures a little—looks for a stable, balanced, healthy, good man to get married and have children with. Females are biologically programmed to want to select a mate that provides their children with the greatest chance of survival. A guy who sleeps around, gets drunk, and hangs out with his deadbeat buddies all the time does not provide that stability.

The problem, of course, is that for a variety of reasons, a lot of women's "pickers" are messed up. They choose the wrong guy or hang their hat on a bad guy hoping to change him. But men—in general—don't change much. By the time a woman has figured that out, she's usually invested her best years in a loser and brought a couple of children into the mix. (Problematically the children end up fatherless and the cycle repeats itself for another generation.)

But I look at many of the young men I've seen grow up in the church who had good parents. They are good young men. Most of them may not be much to look at, but by golly they all seem to have stunningly attractive wives (they all married way "up"). Coincidence? Probably not. If you are a young single guy reading this—stay strong. Keep being a good man even if it's frustrating. The right woman will eventually come along and think you are perfect just the way you are. She will appreciate those qualities of integrity, compassion, and quiet strength that everyone took for granted in the past. Look for a girl who had a good relationship with her father—not one you want to rescue.

Same if you are a young single woman. Maintain your high standards. Be choosy—don't settle. The character standards you maintain for yourself should be a yardstick for any men who want to date you. Look for a man you can respect and are willing to grow together with.

Needs of Older Men

Nearly all men eventually face the "oblivion" of retirement. When a man retires after a lifetime of work that gave his life meaning, he loses influence and often his purpose in life. Oftentimes a man under these circumstances just sits and waits to die. Work was his identity and without it he is helpless and unnecessary. He loses all his power (which matters a lot) and becomes irrelevant to the world. Younger men no longer fear him and young women no longer "want" him.

An elderly man once told me the worst thing about growing old for a man is when other men no longer think of him as dangerous and women no longer think about him at all. He said the second worst thing about growing old is you are still attracted to young women—but can't do anything about it.

I've thought about those statements a lot over the years. I think it will be very difficult to be an old man as I will lose so much of what defined me as a man—the things I have used to dictate (at least in my mind) whether I was a man or not. In fact the very things I have enjoyed most about being a man. Things like strength (power and danger), sexuality (attractiveness to women), and the power to have people listen merely by opening my mouth will all be gone or have faded. I fear being irrelevant. After all, the urge to procreate is a powerful need within a man—placed within him by God himself. Once the urge or ability is gone, a significant portion of a man's self-image has now vanished.

The power of a man's strength is something we view with a skewed lens in our culture. We mock (or glorify) the macho image of a Rambo-like character who maims and kills anyone who gets in his way. But while not as necessary as it once was to survive, a man and his physical strength are still vital to society, even beyond the relatively rare cases of combat to protect our freedoms or policing the line between civilization and chaos. The truth is that as a father and a husband I have relied on my strength over the years to protect my wife and children. There was never a question as to whether my strength (emotional, mental, and physical) was adequate to protect them from nearly any situation or circumstance.

Predators generally avoid the strong and seek the weak or sick to prey upon. My family relied upon this and felt protected and safe under the shield of my masculinity.

Now as I reach my midfifties and beyond, that strength, while not gone yet, is fading. I'm seeing cracks in the facade. Despite my most heroic attempts to stay in good physical condition and maintain my strength, it is slipping away like a thief in the night. My stamina is nowhere near what it once was, and my balance is often questionable. Things I used to pick up without a second thought now cause me to reconsider as the thought of a hernia or hurting my back are not such attractive propositions.

Older men need to find something that adds value to their lives—something that gives meaning and usefulness. For instance, an older man's lifetime of experience is invaluable to children and young adults, yet our culture does not value it. Without that "being necessary" component, older men do not do very well. The question I and many other men ask ourselves is, "Once my masculine strength is gone, *will I be needed anymore?* "Because once a man is not needed, he may as well be dead.

Emotional Needs of Men

Most men don't understand what emotions they are feeling, much less how to process them. Because of that, most men aren't even aware of what their emotional needs are. One man put it this way:

> Women seem to deal with their emotions very differently than men. I don't fully understand women, but from my observations, being married for twenty years, they feel, then

react emotionally and they're done. Men are not so simple. We deny feelings then try not to react, but if we do react then we generally think about what the proper reaction should be according to the situation. Once we do react though, it's not over. Depending on the situation, we can keep that emotional event hidden in our hearts for decades without ever letting anyone know it's still there.[1]

I am always uncomfortable in emotional situations. I never know how I'm supposed to act or respond. So I frequently end up making inappropriate or stupid comments at events like funerals, hospital visits, or even weddings. My baby sister was killed in a drunk-driving accident in 1981, two months before our wedding. I literally remember thinking, *How am I supposed to react? What's the appropriate emotional response to this situation? How do I act at the funeral?* It was all very confusing and so I just stuffed all my emotions. I wrestled them into a too-small container (like mashing a sleeping bag into a stuff-sack) and tightly strapped them down so they couldn't escape. For years I never talked about it or experienced my grief. This of course was damaging to my mental and emotional health. If a man goes through enough of these kinds of emotional events and experiences and does not know how to process his emotions, it will take a toll on his emotional and mental stability. It may be one reason why men have higher rates of high blood pressure and heart disease (and die earlier) than women.

Biologically males are at a disadvantage when it comes to processing their emotions. The male body does not produce as many or as high a concentration of the hormones that contribute to complex social bonding, such as oxytocin, serotonin, and progesterone. The female brain secretes more oxytocin than the male's. This means she has a greater capacity to care for and nurture others. When a female hears a baby cry, her body releases oxytocin, which produces a maternal instinct and causes her to want to hold the baby (which then causes more oxytocin to be released). We all get a warm, fuzzy feeling from watching a video clip of a baby laughing, but women get even more of a bonding "rush" from the hormones it produces. The two hemispheres of the female brain are also designed to communicate more effectively, allowing her to process hard emotive data better than males. The female brain has developed and is equipped for taking care of children, requiring emotive skills. In contrast, male brains have developed mainly for hunting and other spatial activities like building and designing.[2]

Because of the biological disadvantages males have in processing and understanding their emotions, it is often difficult for males to verbally communicate what they are feeling. But many males will express their emotions through their actions. For instance, they may not be able to apologize but will do something to try to make up for it like putting gas in your car (my wife just received "doghouse" flowers and got her car cleaned inside and out).

Men might not understand all of their emotions, but the one emotion they are pretty comfortable with is anger. Anger is a good friend to many men. It protects us (it keeps people from harming us physically and emotionally); it gives us strength (anger causes an increase of heart rate and blood pressure, as well as the release of hormones such as adrenaline and other chemicals that give us greater physical strength);and it gives us power over other people (people are afraid of angry men).

I was an angry young man for many years. I wasn't really angry, I was very wounded and just wanted to be left alone and not hurt anymore. My anger kept people from getting too close and hurting me, but it also kept people from loving me—which was what I really needed and wanted. The very thing I needed in order to heal was the thing I rejected from people.

Here is a powerful look at the inside of many men's emotional life:

> Truthfully, I'm much more comfortable with anger or rage than almost any other emotion. It's because I've lived in that state for most of my life. When it comes upon me, I feel like a long lost friend is back for a visit. Sometimes I welcome him and bask in the sense of power and fury he lends me. Then I remember that he is a traitor and will always turn on me in the end.[3]

Whenever we as a society chastise men and boys for not showing more emotion and feelings, we usually just mean that we do not want them to show anger and aggression. Strong emotions in males are generally inconvenient both for them and for those around them. Women often complain they want men to be more sensitive and in touch with their emotions, yet sensitive men tell me they have a hard time attracting a woman for more than just friendship's sake. It's a double-edged sword in that a woman's words seldom correspond to her actions in this area. Since men believe actions over words, they tend not to believe women when they say they want men to be emotionally sensitive. Prevailing beliefs tell us that men do not like emotions. That may be true, but interestingly men who become healthy enough to understand their emotions and express their emotional needs tell me they feel better and have better relationships with their wives and children.

Perhaps the challenge is not stopping men from being aggressive (or even angry) but helping them learn to express their emotions in a healthy manner. Some of that anger stems from the frustration of not being understood. We need to remember as a culture that male anger is not a crime nor is it a mental illness. Sometimes it's an appropriate response to a particular situation or circumstance.

Men—it's very difficult to be intimate and get your intimacy needs met by another person if you cannot both recognize and articulate what you are feeling and what you need emotionally (especially if you are angry all the time). What does that take? It takes the willingness to be vulnerable enough to explore what you are feeling, what caused it, and why. It also requires of us the sometimes painful experience of being introspective in examining our past and how it causes us to react the way we do to certain issues. Most men I know are more comfortable with physical pain than emotional pain. I'd much rather bust my knuckles on an engine block than go back through how I felt when a guy showed up at my door at 6:00 a. m. and told me my baby sister had just been killed in a car wreck. But busting my knuckles doesn't cause me to hold back my love in fear of losing someone close to me the way the other incident does. If you don't heal, you can't love. If you can't love, you can't fulfill your wife's needs. And that leads to a whole bunch of bad problems. It's a vicious cycle and you are the only one who can break it. Have the courage to step up and face it like a man. Just because we are males doesn't mean we have to be emotionally stunted our entire lives.

All Men's Needs

The two people in life a man most needs approval from are his wife and his father. He yearns for his wife's adoration and admiration and the respect and praise of his father. If he has both, he is blessed. A man can live with just one or the other. But when a man does not get either, he struggles mightily. Oftentimes the two go hand in hand. When a man gets the blessing from his father, it's more likely he will act in a way that would garner respect from his wife, and vice versa.

Men need to accomplish things in life. But when men accomplish their goals in life—rise to the top of their industry, become wealthy, even retire at an early age—they tend to get complacent. They lose focus and don't do very well. They start making poor choices, especially if they do not have anyone they are accountable to, and end up destroying their lives and those around them. Tiger Woods and General David Petraeus are recent examples of men who reached the top of their field and then self-destructed.

Men also need to be recognized for their efforts and accomplishments. Psychiatrist, author, and speaker Dr. Scott Haltzman says, "They [men] want to be acknowledged for their achievements. They like people to connect with them on the basis of what they've done to make the world (or at least their home) a better place."[4] If your husband is grouchy or moping around the house, try giving him an "attaboy" or a pat on the back and see how quickly he perks up. Not surprisingly, men respond well to positive feedback. If you want more attention from him, try being effusive in your response when he does compliment you. You'll soon find he will compliment you much more often.[5]

Men tend to desire comfort, peace, serenity—no rough edges in life. But the easy way out of life is really the hard way. You'll eventually regret following the path of least resistance and living a life of complacency and passivity. Following the path and battles of life that God has for you is difficult. Ask anyone in full-time ministry.

But men need to do hard things in life. It challenges them and grows them to pit themselves against difficult circumstances and come out on top. Since most of the really difficult physical challenges have been eradicated in our modern culture, we have had to invent some.

I recently competed in a Warrior Dash event. This is a five-kilometer race through mud and rugged terrain with twelve man-made obstacles throughout the course. At my age I wasn't really competing so much as just hoping not to embarrass myself. But pitting myself against a significant physical challenge was extremely rewarding—not so much physically maybe (I hurt for a week afterward), but certainly psychologically and even emotionally as it fulfilled a need to challenge myself. Challenges like this help me develop the self-discipline and intestinal fortitude to persevere through difficult times in my marriage and even financially difficult times.

Much has also been made about a male's need for respect, especially from his wife. Men today are starving for the respect and admiration of their women. Unfortunately, the war on masculinity in this country the past several decades has decimated the male population. Since it's a portion of the female population (radical feminists) who are probably most responsible for the devaluing of males in our culture, it will probably be up to females to revalue men in our culture.

If you are the mother of a son, you should be very worried about this issue. Boys and young men in our culture are failing desperately. They are far behind females in educational outcomes, with more boys dropping out of high school than ever before. Attendance in college currently runs about 60 percent female and 40 percent male, with graduate school having an even wider gap. Undereducated young males are unemployed and underemployed with little hope of finding a livable wage job. If you are the mom of a daughter, you should be likewise as alarmed. Young women already struggle to find men who can match their education levels and achievements. The question on the minds of many young women is, "Where are all the good men?" The good men are gone because they were abandoned by their fathers as boys and left to the influences of video games and pornography that have sapped their masculine strength and turned them into passive, apathetic, feminized doppelgangers of a man.

Obviously, not all the good men are gone. There is still a small contingent of passionate, strong, and faithful men who are the backbone of our nation. But that group is shrinking with each generation, and we see the results of their demise in our culture every day.

His Needs in Marriage

Ladies, the list inside your head about what kind of woman and wife you should be is not the same list as is in your husband's head. In fact, it's likely that none of the things you think are "absolutes" about what a man finds attractive or necessary in a wife are even on your husband's list. Likely your list is much more complicated and difficult to live up to than your husband's needs and desires.

For instance, despite what many women think, men don't want a "trophy" wife or someone to just feed us or take care of us when we're sick. It's not even about sex, even though sexuality *is* an important part of relationships.

What men *really* want and need in a relationship is a safe place to recharge and renew themselves in order to go back out and face the world and "fight the good fight." What men want is a safe, secure, stress-free environment where they can recover from dealing with the rat race and just relax. What men want is a place where we can be ourselves, without putting on the facade that the world sometimes demands. We want a place where we don't have to be on our best behavior, where we don't have to walk on eggshells, and where we don't have to pretend that we're something we're not.

Unfortunately, by not being a guy with the situational advantages described above means we can sometimes be ugly and brutish. From a woman's perspective, that's not the guy she married.

Companionship

Men often equate intimacy with companionship. Perhaps because males bond from doing things together (generally physical activities), they feel closer to their wives when they accompany them on adventures. This can be as simple as going to the car show or as complicated as going wilderness camping together. This bond that occurs between a man and his companion works with his children as well as with his friends. While it's important for husbands and wives to have their own hobbies and friends to enjoy, it's just as important for a woman to understand that her husband really would like to go to the ball game sometimes with her more than he would with his buddies.

One reason men are uncomfortable with intimacy is because it makes them feel uncomfortable. That sounds overly simplistic, but it's true. Men are uncomfortable with being intimate because intimacy requires a man to lower his guard and be emotionally vulnerable—something he is biologically and environmentally programmed to avoid at all costs. However, doing things together is a simple way to bridge that gap and create intimacy with him in a way he enjoys and is comfortable with. He may be much more willing to fulfill your needs for intimacy in the way you need (talking, communication, nonsexual affection, etc.) if he is feeling some level of being intimate with you already. For instance, I love to talk with my wife during our evening walks, but not so much sitting eye to eye across the kitchen table from her.

The greatest temptation in a man's life is comfort. Men were made to live a life of action and adventure. God has greater plans for your life than playing video games, my friend. A man craves comfort and peace, but when he gets too comfortable he becomes bored and restless. That's when many men get into trouble. Like a bored child they seek adventure often in

---

Knowing Your Husband: What Makes Him Tick?

What/who is your husband's . . .

Favorite car (in the whole world)?
Favorite color?
Favorite relative?
Favorite band?
Favorite sports team?
Dream place to visit?

---

the wrong places. Ladies, make sure your man has something to keep his mind and body occupied. While he does need to decompress by fire-gazing at the television from time to time, men who vegetate on the couch too much seldom accomplish much in life. That leads them to have regrets later in life, at just about the time they are wondering, "Is this all there is to life?" Many men then experience what we term a *midlife crisis* and make stupid choices in life.

Finally, ladies, don't tell your friends about your marital problems. It just builds resentment. Your husband will resent it when he finds out you shared personal issues with other people, and it creates resentment toward your husband in your friends. For a man this is also a matter of respect. He doesn't feel respected when you share your personal problems with other people. Respect is a fundamental need for a man. It saturates his entire life and your relationship, even when arguing. Speaking of which, we need to validate each other's forms of expressing frustration. Men and women don't respond in the same way. Author and speaker Shaunti Feldhahn says this about the way men and women argue:

> Ladies, if you think crying when feeling unloved is an acceptable response during a relational conflict, would you be surprised to know that anger is often a man's response to feeling disrespected during relational conflict? . . . Before we clobber the guys about the need for Anger Management 101 let's put this in perspective. We feel we deserve the right to cry without being accused of being manipulative or disregarded as a basket case. But when our man expresses anger in his communication during a conflict (in response to feeling disrespected) we often treat him as if he's broken all the "rules of engagement" for relational conflict.[6]

And lastly, women have the ability to not only create life in their wombs, but to sustain life in the people they love. The power of a woman is phenomenal. In fact, many men are intimidated by it. A woman's words or even her attitude can either destroy a man or empower him to greatness. Their actions and loving touch can heal physical wounds and psychological wounds alike.

Always remember a woman's words have the power to either destroy or to heal. How you choose to use them is a direct reflection of your character.

Roles of a Man

Men have a number of inherent roles that they need to fulfill in life in order to feel comfortable with who they are. By fulfilling these roles, a man is actually being very intimate with those he loves. It's a nonverbal way of being intimate, but no less compelling and powerful to a man. Two of the most vital of these roles are *protector* and *provisioner*.

Protector

Last winter as my wife was going to work one morning, she slipped on the icy porch steps and landed rather dramatically on her backside and shoulder. As I came running out to see what had happened, she continued to lie on the ground crying until we assessed if she was seriously injured or not. Thankfully, she only had some minor bruises. However, she stayed home from work that day and cried off and on for several hours. When I asked her why she was still crying, she said it was because she had been so scared. She went on to say that for the entire time we have been married, she had only truly been afraid for her physical well-being twice: once when she was rear-ended in a car accident, and that recent incident on the porch steps. I responded by saying, "Well, if those are the only times in the last thirty-two years you've been afraid, that's a pretty good testament." She looked me in the eye and gratefully said, "Yes, you have done a really good job of protecting me." Fear was such an unknown emotion to her that experiencing it shook her to the core.

I hadn't consciously thought of it before, but that's a big part of my role as a husband—protecting my wife. I need to protect her not only from physical harm but also emotional and psychological harm (or even the threats of harm) whenever possible. Certainly if I cannot protect her from those things, I can be supportive, encouraging, and sympathetic when she does get wounded by life and other humans.

In fact, everyone and everything—wife, kids, cats, dogs, once even a bird—that have lived under my roof have lived under my protection and lived as safe and as good a life as I was able to provide. No harm befell them. The biggest threat they faced were my own dysfunctions. I don't say this as a matter of pride but as a matter of fact. It is my most urgent duty as a man that if I create a life or take responsibility for the welfare of one, I am compelled to do everything within my power to ensure that he or she lives a life of safety, health, and well-being (and trust me, we've had some pets that we provided for more out of obligation than love until they expired of natural causes).

As protector, the husband's role is to provide cover—to take the brunt of life. One of the effects we see in single moms is that they are beaten down by life. They have to face life and all its problems by themselves. They have no one to help them share the responsibilities, make decisions, enforce rules, or do chores. I even hear ultrafeminist women complain about having to bear all the burdens of life—having to make *all* the decisions.

I suspect that most women enjoy having someone to protect them from the harsher aspects of life. One delightful young married couple was telling me the story of how they met. She explained that they both worked in a restaurant, but she did not care for him at all. One night she was accosted in the storeroom by another co-worker. The young husband-to-be happened by and immediately leaped to her rescue, badly thrashing the attacker. Suddenly, he was much less repulsive to her. As she told me with a sparkle in her eyes, "He rescued me! Oh my, he rescued me! He was my knight in shining armor!"

For men to fulfill this role requires us to have vision in life and leads us to the next section—being a provisioner.

Provisioner

Awhile back Suzanne and I were sitting in the turn lane at a stoplight of a major thoroughfare. As is my habit, I was pretty aware of what was going on around me. For instance, I subconsciously knew that no car was behind us. As I watched the heavy traffic in front of me, a scene played out almost in slow motion. I saw a little old lady start to make a left-hand turn across traffic toward us. Unfortunately for her, the turn lane light was not green. I shouted, "There's going to be an accident!" and shoved the car into reverse, rapidly backing away from the scene over Suzanne's startled gasps of surprise. Sure enough, a fast-moving car slammed into the little old lady, plowing her car into the exact position our car had been in seconds before. I then flipped on the hazard lights and jumped out to see how the elderly lady was. After assessing she was uninjured, I led her across traffic to the sidewalk and left her with Suzanne while I drove her car and then mine off to the side of the road out of heavy traffic.

The point of the story is not to suggest that I am some sort of hero, but it is about how impressed Suzanne was with my response under stress. She has marveled even months later about the incident and how I was able to foresee the entire scenario and respond in a way that protected us and then calmly helped others. But I cannot take credit for my actions. I was operating on autopilot. I wasn't hypervigilant; I was merely functioning as a man. Men are often capable of seeing the consequences of events before they happen, which allows us to take action to protect those under our charge. Thousands of years of being in that role have developed within us a "second sense" that anticipates danger and compels us to take action.

That incident falls under the role of protector, but it also illustrates the man's role as provisioner. A provisioner does not just provide materially for those under his purview/safeguard. While providing for the material needs (food, shelter, clothing, etc.) of his charges is part of the role, this responsibility goes even deeper. It also involves anticipating possible or expected future needs and then providing for those needs, whether they are material, emotional, psychological, or physical. It means as a man having a "pro-vision"—the ability to see beyond today's circumstances and into the future. Such needs might include the more obvious, such as college funds for the kids, money for your daughter's wedding, or retirement savings. Or they might be more intangible, such as anticipating (even before she does) your wife's unspoken need to go back to college to finish a degree at some point and having the funds and your schedule arranged to allow it to happen. Or anticipating that your children may go through dangerous activities during adolescence such as drugs, eating disorders, or self-harm and educating yourself beforehand so that you are prepared to deal with them effectively *before* they happen. Being a provisioner means, as a man, that you are not stupid—even if our society expects you to be.

Intimacy-Building Tips for Fulfilling a Man's Needs

- Does your husband feel "needed"? He needs to—badly.
- Does he feel appreciated, respected, admired especially by you? Women who respect and admire their husbands not only have happier husbands, they have better marriages.
- Do you spend time with him at places he feels comfortable? Companionship is high on a man's list for bonding. Ask him out of the blue to take you to the ball game or auto show (or whatever activity he enjoys that you wouldn't normally go to with him). My wife went to the gun show with me last year—it was the most fun of any I've ever been to.
- Let him know frequently that he is important to your life as a provider and protector (even if you make more money than he does). These are core components of a man's psyche (even if he doesn't know it) and need to be acknowledged by the important woman in his life. Many men have shared with me they were lured away from their wives (now their "ex-es") by women who appreciated them more.

8

Her Needs (for Him)

> Just about every woman he had met who
> was worth anything thought that she was
> ugly. It was some kind of mass delusion.
>
> —Thomas Perry, *Sleeping Dogs*

When men want to understand something, they find out as much as they can about it. For instance, if something needs to be repaired or we want to figure out how something works, the first thing men generally do is to take it apart (physically or mentally). We break it down into its components, then determine the logical sequence leading to its operation. We typically do this in a linear and chronological order. How does it operate? Why does it work the way it does? If this part connects to this part, what happens?

Even in our relationships we like a logical sequence of events to give orderliness and stability to our perspective. How does this person think? What kind of feelings does he/she have and how do they express themselves? What makes this person tick? We use sort of an "if I do this, then this will happen" approach.

While our wives are not machinery (and certainly don't need to be "fixed"), it might be helpful to first look at the different components of a woman in order to help understand her better. Perhaps if we break down her differing aspects, we can get a glimpse inside her and understand better how she operates.

Her Need for Your Love

Many women do not place as much importance on material goods as they do relational gifts. Express your love for her verbally. She needs to hear those words frequently.

My wife has a need to know that I love her. She needs to be reassured of that often. If I am not giving her words that confirm my love or showing her through my deeds often enough that I love her, she will become *needy*. This isn't the moping-around, desperate-for-compliments kind of needy, but more like a plant-that-hasn't-been-watered-for-a-while needy. Sometimes (maybe in desperation?) she will ask me for a favor to test my love. I'm not sure if this is a conscious act as much as it is instinctual. The favor isn't actually something that's needed as much as it is tangible evidence of my love. Usually there is something within my male psyche that causes me to resist giving my wife something I think she expects. I might even resent the whole thing if I think it is a test to prove my love more than a legitimate need. For instance, if she hints around about a task—even if I've already thought about doing it—I might be compelled to put it aside for a while. This might be something simple like hinting around about a birthday present or going out to dinner. It might also entail something around the house like asking me to change out the exhaust fan in the bathroom (note: not as simple a task as one might first assume). Her need for proof of my love runs counter to my masculine nature not to give in to such requests. Unfortunately, her asking me to do something before I can accomplish it on my own takes away my joy of having thought of it as a gift to her—it ruins the surprise, so to speak.

When she has to ask for evidence that I love her, it ruins it for her as well. She believes that "if he really loved me, he'd know what I needed and I wouldn't have to ask for it." Of course as a male I am not wired to be capable of thinking that way, and so if I am unaware of her needs, I have a small chance of intuiting what they are on my own.

This "asking for evidence that I love her" means that I am not doing well in my job as a husband to treat her in an honoring and loving way. To fulfill her need to be loved, she needs to be cherished. The easiest way to cherish her is to treat her like a precious gift. There's an old adage that says, "Treat her like a queen and she will act like one." If you place a high value on a person, they will grow to be that person. We see that in stories about teachers who didn't know that they had a class of students who were failures. They inadvertently place high expectations upon them and the students fulfill those expectations.

The story of Johnny Lingo illustrates this concept brilliantly. Johnny Lingo was a Polynesian trader who wanted to marry a young woman named Mahana. This particular young woman was considered by everyone (including her father) to be sullen, angry, and of little value. Her father considered her to be worth only one cow. As a bargaining chip, her father asks Lingo for three cows for the hand of his daughter. Everyone laughs derisively at his presumptuousness, believing Johnny Lingo would reconsider the deal and leave. But Lingo considers and says, "Three cows are many . . . but not enough for my Mahana!" He then offers the unheard of price of *eight* cows for her. He and Mahana soon get married and leave the island on a trading trip.

When they return, to everyone's astonishment, Mahana is a beautiful, happy woman. Even her father begins to feel like he had been cheated by only getting eight cows for her. Johnny Lingo had proven to her that her true worth had nothing to do with what others saw, but what she truly was. But Johnny got the best bargain—for a few cows he had found a wonderful wife with whom to spend his life.[1]

Many women need the man in their lives to prove his love for her by making sacrifices. Has your wife ever playfully asked you if you would give up something for her? It's a fun game that young lovers play, but at the root is a woman's insecurity over her man's love for her.

The thing all women want to know is, "Does he still love me?" With men, our actions always speak louder than our words do. For instance, what we *do* always speaks louder than what we *say*. All men know you judge a man by his actions not his words. Men only spend time doing things they care about, regardless of what they may say. If we love something (fishing, hunting, fixing up old cars, etc.), we spend time on it. If we don't like something (going to church, shopping, cooking, cleaning house, etc.), we don't spend any more time than necessary doing it. So if we *say* we love our wives but don't spend any time with them, we are sending a mixed message.

Fortunately for men, women tend to believe a man's words more than his actions. For instance, women generally believe what a man says regardless of his actions. Perhaps because women value verbal communication to a greater degree than men do, they have a propensity to believe what is said to them. I know many women who have chosen to believe a man's words over his actions and are paying the price for that choice today. They are also wired to want and need to hear specific words. They need to frequently hear that they are loved and cherished. Expressions of love counter the continuous program running through their mind that questions their worth, value, beauty, and lovableness.

That means spending time doing things *she* likes to do. I offered to give up watching the ball game yesterday to go to a wholesale warehouse with my wife. The fact that the Cardinals were leading the Dodgers 12–1 in the top of the ninth inning had nothing to do with this supreme sacrifice, but that's not the point to the story. She loves shopping at this store, but I hate it—it's crowded, people are pushy, and I always spend more money than I need to there. Besides, they don't sell my books there, which is a constant source of irritation to me. But I manned up and accompanied her on her hunting and gathering foray because that's what she likes to do. Would I have preferred vegetating in my recliner in front of the ball game? Yes. Did I get points for going with her? Absolutely.

Just like many men have a continual subconscious fear of being found inadequate or incompetent that plays into our core self-image, women also have a prerecorded program running through their minds. They constantly question whether they are valued and wanted.

Here is how one woman put it: "I wish he knew that the way I see myself is linked closely to how he sees me. If he thinks I'm the greatest thing, then my self-esteem soars. In turn it makes me want to be the best wife I can to him. On the other hand, if he downgrades me, my self-esteem seems to suffer. I find it harder to be the wife he would like because I feel like I can't please him, so why try."

Occasionally I will make an offhanded remark to my wife complimenting her on something I think is obvious. But from her reaction you'd have thought I presented her with a diamond necklace. She glows and stammers about how much that means to her and how happy it makes her that I feel that way. You'd think I never compliment her (hmmm).

Will He Fight for My Heart?

Would you be willing to fight for your wife to defend her honor? Would you even be willing to die for her? Most men would, I think. But the question is, does your wife know that or do you just take it for granted that it's understood?

There are various ways of defending your wife without rushing in and physically fighting someone—although there might be times when a man has to physically defend his wife's honor. In fact jumping in and yelling at her boss for treating her poorly is probably just the opposite of defending her—it's implying she can't handle her own problems. But it might mean not allowing her to be influenced by people who are destructive or have emotional ill will toward her. Sometimes parents, relatives, or even friends can be negative influences.

Fight for Me

Walk with me through the tough areas of our life, don't run away and think it will go away. Fight for me like you did when you wooed me. I am still your princess and you are my knight in shining armor, although there are a few rust spots now. Encourage me to be better at being a wife, a mom, a daughter, a daughter-in-law, a volunteer. Love me when I am hormonal. Stand up to our children when they are disrespecting me and call them on it, giving out the right punishments. Join me at the school conferences when our child has good and bad things happen. Notice the little things like the haircuts, the clean floors, the new outfit, the jewelry that you purchased for me. Help me see the beauty in myself that I don't see because of the beatings in my mind that I give myself. Help me believe that I can do more than I was or thought I could. Pray for me and walk with me in prayer and with God so that we truly can be what our wedding verse says.

—Anonymous Wife

When people criticize her to her face or behind her back, or take advantage of her, that's when a husband needs to defend his wife. Even (maybe especially) if it's your own mother doing the criticizing, you need to step in and defend her. Allowing your mother to berate your wife is a severe form of betrayal. Your wife is the woman you have chosen to spend your life with and to bear your children. Not only does it set a bad example to your children to allow your mother (or father) to interfere in your marriage, it also is most often cowardly. There are probably also times when it is important to defend her from her own father or mother as well.

Another way of fighting for her is lifting her up when she can't lift herself. Maybe she is suffering from postpartum depression after having had your child. She's not fun to be around and you don't think things will ever get better. That's the time a man needs to fight for his woman by making sure she gets proper medical care, medication (if needed), plenty of rest, and the positive support of friends and family. To get petulant and pout about not getting your needs met in that circumstance (even if it has been a long time and it is miserable) would be like running away when she needs you to defend and fight for her the most.

Many times we would not have a problem defending our wives physically, but if it requires an emotional or long-term sacrifice, it seems too daunting to contemplate. But in today's world, those may be the things she needs from you most. In fact in today's world those may be the only things a guy has to "fight" for.

Struggles Women Face

I confess I don't have a handle on the trials that most women face. But as I understand it, most women (either at one time or another or, for some, most of the time) feel fat, ugly, stupid, inept, or some combination of all the above. Frequently the women who have the least amount of reason to feel that way suffer from those insecurities the most. Nevertheless, most women appear to place at least some amount of self-worth and value upon their physical appearance. A recent study confirms that women's low perception of themselves is nearly universal: "Harvard University professor Nancy Etcoff and London School of Economics professor Susie Orbach surveyed thousands of women internationally to find that only 4 percent of women think they are beautiful."[2]

While many men probably secretly feel incompetent from time to time, as a gender we don't seem to suffer the same level of low self-esteem or self-value as females. Women beat themselves up about perceived imperfections in their physical appearance or psyche. Much of this self-flagellation seems to be internally driven, although words of criticism cut deep into the heart of a woman. Even women who should know they are beautiful (just look in the mirror, for goodness' sake) or competent (look at all your accomplishments) are knocked off-kilter by the most innocent of critiques, causing them to question their own worthiness. And words deliberately spoken in malice can be devastating to their sense of value.

Perhaps because men tend to develop their self-esteem through accomplishments and not relationships, they are somewhat immune to the opinions of others—or else just don't care.

When I was a much younger man, I made the mistake of suggesting to my wife that it wouldn't hurt if she lost a few pounds. After all, I'd want to know if I was gaining too much weight or if my clothes were starting to fit a little too snugly. In fact you'd be doing me a favor if you told me a certain shirt or pair of pants made me look heavy. But did my wife appreciate my honest and forthright assessment? No, of course not. What do you think her response was? Well, if you've ever watched a female praying mantis methodically and deftly remove the head of its male counterpart, you know how I felt. She then disemboweled me with surgical precision. I felt like I'd just woken up after having had a spleenectomy. It's a mistake I haven't made too many times since.

The truth is that my spoken criticism of her looks, body, or appearance represents words that cannot be easily forgiven or forgotten. These words cut too close to the core of her being.

The closest example I can think of is if your wife called you incompetent as a provider and inadequate in the bedroom. Even then I suspect that the wounds inflicted by a husband's critical comments of his wife's appearance are deeper and more jagged than anything she could say to us.

Beauty is at the heart of all womanhood. God made the female face and body to be adored and even lusted after by the male of the species. All women want to know they are beautiful. Even more than want, they *need* to know they are desired and beautiful. Women develop their self-esteem through their relationships and their physical appearance. God created each woman naturally beautiful.

So it only makes sense that the one area where Satan would attack women would be in their need to feel beautiful. The most effective strategy he can come up with is to cause women to dislike and even hate themselves. It makes women and girls feel bad about who they are as human beings. When they feel bad about themselves, it impairs their ability to use their tremendous power to nurture the lives of others. By focusing strictly upon their outward appearance, it prevents them from relishing their inward beauty—the beauty God gave them to love, nourish, and empower others. It is a distraction the evil one uses to full advantage.

Despite being created as the glory of God's creation, nearly every woman on the planet seems to struggle with these self-image issues or lack of esteem stemming from their looks or body. They have a skewed image of what they look like. Even the most beautiful women (maybe *especially* the most physically attractive) feel bad about themselves. I know several gorgeous women (inside and out) who are nearly crippled by this perverted perspective of their appearance. It causes them to lack confidence, to feel ashamed, and to be "less than" they are designed to be. It prevents them from using the miraculous power God gave women to help others thrive and flourish.

Your wife desperately needs to know she is beautiful, especially in your eyes. In fact, your eyes are the only ones that count to her. I know of men married to women who might be considered very plain looking who have convinced their wives that they are beautiful. These women are confident and self-assured—and very happy. Unlike women who fall apart when anyone else even remotely criticizes their appearance, it doesn't matter what anyone says to these women because they are confident in their heart that their husband finds them gorgeous and that gives them contentment and peace. Other physically beautiful women who have been emotionally and psychologically abused by their father or lovers (especially their husband) feel ugly and unworthy of love. And what women *feel* is what they believe to be true.

I see my wife when she looks gorgeous and other times when she looks slightly less than glamorous. Yet I always seem more ready to comment on the negative aspects of her appearance than on the positive. Sometimes the light will catch her just right or her inner beauty will burst through onto her face and I am stunned at her natural loveliness. But I am almost always speechless, never knowing how to articulate that. Yet those are the times she most needs to hear those words.

Tell your wife everyday she is beautiful—and mean it. You will have a happy wife. And a happy wife means a happy man and a happy home.

What Women Want

What Women Want: To be loved, to be listened to, to be desired, to be respected, to be needed, to be trusted, and sometimes, just to be held.

What Men Want: Tickets for the World Series.

—Dave Barry

Our culture seems to have propagated upon many women the innate expectation that the world revolves around them and their happiness. Some women seem to feel it is a man's job to make them happy and satisfied (some men probably feel it is their wives' job as well). The truth is that no man (or child, or other woman, or job, or house) can make a woman happy. Contentment comes from within. When a woman grows to the point that she recognizes that, she can then get on with figuring out what she wants out of life and striving toward those goals. Many women don't know what they want. They just have a yen or itch for *something*, but they don't know what. There's an old saying, "What do women want? They don't know, but if they don't have it, they'll get angry." Women like that tend to make those around them miserable because they are always expecting others to fulfill their needs, yet can't express what they are.

Most men I know feel that the women in their lives are at least somewhat dissatisfied. Why aren't women in the United States more grateful? They live the most privileged, healthy, choice-filled lives in the history of the world, and yet they continually fantasize and yearn for "more." They want it all. They want a great career and a close-knit family. Here's the truth. You can't have it all. You have to make sacrifices. Life is about tradeoffs—no one has everything. And the myth that some women "have it all"? It's a lie.

I suspect women in the workplace are finally figuring out what men have known for a long time—you can't have everything. The only thing that is equal in every person is the amount of time they have in a day. If you are going to be highly successful in your career, it will require you to work longer and harder than your peers. That means you will be forced to take time away from your family. You can't expect to be the CEO of a Fortune 500 company and still attend every concert and game your children perform in. If you place a higher importance on being Mother or Father of the Year, your work will suffer. Not only that, but you will take time away from your marriage relationship in order to fulfill whatever personal goals you and your spouse place more importance upon. The challenge each person (and every couple) has to make is how to effectively balance all areas of their lives.

When our children were toddlers, I took the plunge, went out on my own, and started an environmental engineering firm. My wife and I agreed that while I would work hard (especially in the early years) I would also balance the amount of time I spent at work in order to have a healthy relationship with my kids and with each other. That meant that my company was not going to grow as big as it might have and we would not have as much money as it may have been possible to earn. That company provided us a decent living for sixteen years before I became a full-time writer and speaker. I never got wealthy (which might have been an attractive goal to me), but I did spend an ample amount of time with my family. It required both my wife and I recognizing our goals and then realizing the consequences of those choices. Had we not voiced those expectations openly with each other, it would have been easy to get sidetracked with individual goals and dreams that might have been destructive to our family. It would have been unfair for me to agree to our pact and then go off and try to grow the business into a large company. Likewise, it would have been unfair for my wife to agree to this commitment, then later become discontented with the amount of money I earned.

Women today are under a great amount of stress (much of it self-induced). Research shows that women hold on to stress longer and that the effects of stress are more extreme for women than men. Women release more chemicals, with these hormones staying in their body longer than they do in men's.[3]

Raising a family, working at a job, and maintaining a healthy marriage are all stressful activities, especially when trying to accomplish all three at once. And yet many younger women today, either by choice or necessity, find themselves in the workplace. Many of them, even though having chosen to have a career, appear to hold some amount of resentment toward their husbands that they still *have* to work—especially after children come along.

Other women might be unhappy because they don't get to have a glamorous career and are stuck at home with babies and toddlers and crave adult conversation. Either way, many women seem to harbor at least some amount of discontent or even resentment about their lives.

What Women Need

You don't need a man, you need a champion.

—Felipe in *Eat, Pray, Love*

A woman's biggest fear is being rejected and abandoned. She fears she will be rejected as not being beautiful enough. And she fears if she is accepted, she will be abandoned as not having been worthy enough.

It's been my observation that women need two kinds of love—commitment love and romantic love. She needs to know that a man will be there for her and never desert her. For a woman, "emotional security" and closeness are far more important than financial security.

The other kind of love a woman needs is a tender, soul-stirring, and to her a life-giving love that is rooted in her need to give her love to and be loved by a man. This need is often intense in women and requires continual reassurance and affirmation from her lover. It requires giving her nonsexual physical affection and telling her that she is loved and is beautiful. Women seem to need this kind of love to a greater degree than men. Men don't appear to be as harmed by lack of "intimate" love as a woman. Women who don't get loved often become unhappy and frustrated, their countenance withering.

One way to meet her needs is to study her and know what makes her tick. Then we can begin to help her in ways that are meaningful to her. For instance, my wife is a sensate. She relates to things through her physical senses. She is extremely in touch with her body. She is a physical being and relates to others through touch and her auditory and olfactory senses. She likes to have her fingers and toes in loamy soil and loves gardening. She intuits emotions and problems through her body, heart, and soul—not so much her mind. She is very sensual and responsive to touch. She likes rocks, plants, birds, and flora and fauna of all kinds. Her favorite

Knowing Your Wife: What Makes Her Tick?

What/who is your wife's . . .

Favorite flower?
Favorite color?
Favorite relative?
Favorite song?
Favorite gemstone?
Dream place to visit?

things to do include crabbing, canning food, picking mushrooms, gardening, and gold mining, all of which are forms of reaping or harvesting from the earth. Coming from a background of poverty, she finds this partially satisfies her need to have "things" (food stocks) but also serves to connect her to the earth. My goal is to make sure that I provide opportunities for her to meet these needs whenever possible, as it provides her with peace and satisfaction. For example, she went gold mining in central Oregon this past summer with a friend of hers. While that is not something I was excited to accompany her on, I wholeheartedly supported her leaving for two weeks to do something she so enjoyed.

If I didn't understand her, I might be inclined to try to meet needs for her based on what I like, such as going to the gym (which she hates).

Beyond that, women crave security. I was talking with my young adult daughter the other day about what kind of man she might want to look for when considering marriage. She's been asking me a lot of questions lately about love and what kind of man is a good man. One of the things I talked about was looking for someone who has some financial acumen. Not so much someone who is wealthy or wants to become wealthy as much as someone who has good money management skills. As I told her, most people (her mother and myself included) get married and buy the most expensive house their paychecks allow them to finance. They then spend years struggling. Since financial difficulties are the highest contributing factor in divorce, it would seem more prudent to buy a home within your means and practice saving for future needs and difficulties (which always arise). This would remove a huge amount of stress from a relationship and allow a young couple to grow together without that heavy burden.

One of the things I regret most was getting married and immediately buying a brand-new, very expensive car. This pattern of money mismanagement seemed to follow us for years in our marriage, placing a great deal of stress on our relationship. Since then we have tried to be good stewards of the financial blessings the Lord has bestowed upon us, practicing paying off debt, saving for major expenditures (instead of financing them), and maintaining a savings account (and of course tithing regularly). These steps, in and of themselves, have improved the quality of our marriage.

The choices we have made in the past often impact our future relationships. For instance, a spouse who engages in a one-night stand runs the risk of becoming pregnant with that person. That individual may or may not be stable and healthy, but the child ensures that they will be linked together for the rest of their lives. We know one couple who found themselves in that circumstance, and because a child resulted from that one-night stand, the couple has been forced to spend tens of thousands of dollars in attorney fees and hundreds of hours of emotional turmoil trying to keep this chaotic person from ruining their new family. The truth is, that person will be a specter haunting their lives probably until the day they die.

Understanding Her Needs

> Every woman dreams of her man in terms of the ideal but marries the real.
>
> —Edwin Louis Cole

Men (especially young men) ask me the same question: "Will I ever understand my wife?" My answer is, "No—don't be silly." If men throughout history have not understood their women, why should we be any different? I frequently have to just shake my head as my wife does or says something that seems illogical and unexplainable to me. But that's okay. We don't necessarily have to understand someone to love them. In fact, not understanding our women creates a certain mystique that keeps the magic alive in our relationships. As confounding as I sometimes find my wife, it would be a pretty boring existence to live my life surrounded by a bunch of people who think, act, and behave much like I do in every situation. At the very least, my wife perplexes me frequently enough to keep me on my toes and keep life interesting. Generally, when she's most unpredictable, it's a sign that her needs are not being met.

Some women (and possibly even some men—although I suspect they wouldn't care) would think the following example is manipulation, but here's an email I received regarding one woman's rather simple solution to getting her needs met:

I just finished reading "The Five Love Languages" by Dr. Gary Chapman. I've determined that my hubby's love language and my love language are light years apart. Mine is "Acts of Service" and his is "Physical Touch." As you can imagine from my upbringing (fatherless and non-emotional mother equaled years of bitterness and resentment towards men) we did not show affection, so this physical touch one is difficult for me.

Anyway, I came up with a genius idea that became a win/ win situation for us! Oh you're gonna love this! So my husband had a week vacation left at work he needed to use or lose before the end of the year. So two weeks ago he took a week off from work and told me he would "work on a few things around the house while he was home. "I was GIDDY with excitement, not that my husband was going to be home with me for a week, but because he was going to fix stuff!! Sooooooo, I made a "Honey Do" List for him that consisted of about 23 items. I placed an asterisk by about 10 of them and handed him the list. I told him that I wanted him to work off this list and the ones with stars next to them were ones that I really wanted done. So for every starred item he completed (subject to my inspection of course) he could get a "favor" of his choice from me. :-)

Can I just tell you I have NEVER seen this man work so efficiently before!! He was working his fingers to the bone, and collecting his favors along the way!!! At one point he had done so much from the list, he had favors banked!!! So the week flew by, I got a TON of stuff fixed around the house that I had been stewing over for months, and he got his "release" that you men apparently need and need often . . . lol. We had an amazing week together and we were both in such a great mood. I told my girlfriend about my genius idea and she told her hubby about it. She texted me a few days later and said "My husband is begging me for a honey do list!!"

I know some experts (myself included) have said that women shouldn't use sex for bribery or as a way to manipulate men, but I have to say I can't find anything wrong with her strategy. I ran it by a couple of my male friends and they thought it was a creative idea as well and daydreamed about getting a honey-do list from their wives. I'm not sure it qualifies as manipulation if you are in on it.

Other times, as men, we have to be intuitive about our wives' needs. Many women won't complain about or even mention the things that are most important to them. They might complain about other things though, and a man who knows his wife will understand that this is her way of trying to get a need met. Mostly, I suspect a woman just wants a man who appreciates her and puts her interests ahead of his own.

When I married my wife, I gave her a small (tiny) chip of a diamond ring because that was all I could afford. My plan was to get her a nicer one a few years later. However, like with most things, life got in the way and thirty-one years later I still had not gotten her the big rock I had promised her. She never complained or even mentioned it, but I could see her over the years admiring other women's rings.

Finally this past year I received some financial blessings and I decided to get serious about fulfilling my unspoken promise. I saved a good chunk of money and started doing my homework. Because of the economic downturn, many people have apparently had to sell their nice rings. I was able to purchase a nice diamond ring for about half the appraisal price in a jewelry store.

Seeing the joy and excitement on my wife's face was very satisfying. I felt good that she finally had a token of my love that was worthy of her status as a highly favored wife. But the truth is, it was just as fulfilling for me. I had finally completed a commitment I had made years before and given my wife something she deserved.

Now not only does she not have to be "ashamed" (even if she would never admit it) when other women are showing off their rings, but I'm happy in the fact that it makes her feel good that I desire to lavish her with gifts and that I am a man of my word (although rather belatedly).

Guys, keep an eye on what your wife's needs might be. Likely when she is frustrated, snappy, and even angry, it's because she has a need that is not being fulfilled. If you understand your wife and what her needs are, you'll find it much easier to help her get those needs met. That will ensure that you live a happy and contented existence.

Does He Really Love Me?

One of the most important lessons I learned after I accepted Christ into my heart at forty years of age was this—*you cannot truly love someone else when you don't love yourself.* Accepting God's gift of forgiveness and unconditional love allowed me to forgive myself and to begin liking myself—which then slowly grew into loving myself as the person God had created me to be. Before that, the wounds from childhood and life's experiences kept me so bitter and hurt that I had a protective shell around my heart. I didn't like who I was and so didn't really like many other people either. It kept me from loving and being truly intimate with my wife and children.

I'm sure not all men suffer from this, but I do think many of us have an illness—the disease of self-loathing. Probably most men, to some degree, feel either incompetent or inadequate in various areas of life. Men hate that feeling. We might not admit it out loud—or even to ourselves. But secretly it makes us feel insecure and lose confidence. And when those kinds of feelings surface, we react in anger, defensiveness, and irritation. Those feelings then open the door so the Evil One can whisper destructive words in our ear such as, "*You're a loser. Who do you think you are? You'll never accomplish anything. You can't do this. You're no good.*" Those words echo in our chests, robbing us of our courage, strength, and vitality. Stealing the courage to love our wives unashamedly and with our whole heart, not holding anything back. Draining our strength to lead our family in areas we don't feel adequate.

Do you crave respect from your wife? Do you want her to admire you? How strong are those secret feelings? That's how strong her feelings are of wanting you to love her. She needs to know you love her and only have eyes for her. Not looking at other women may be as difficult for a man as it is for a woman to give unconditional respect to a man—yet both are fundamental needs for the other.

Words are powerful to a woman. Your wife needs to hear the words that you love her. She needs to hear them frequently and in a variety of ways. Besides telling her, flowers and notes show her you are thinking about her when she is not around. That spells love to a woman.

I often end up going to bed later than my wife as I get home late or write late into the night. Even though I'm not the best example of telling my wife I love her during the day, I always crawl into bed, kiss her near her eye, and whisper in her ear, "I love you, sweetheart." Even though half asleep, she often smiles and snuggles in, secure and content in her knowledge of my love for her.

A big way that a woman feels loved is through the faithfulness of her partner. The biggest betrayal a woman can suffer is for her husband to be unfaithful with another woman. Because a woman derives so much of her self-esteem through her relationships (not through accomplishments, like men do), unfaithfulness is tantamount to telling her she is worthless. Men are the more competitive gender of the species, but the area in which women do compete against each other is with their mates. One woman taking another woman's man is a huge insult to her personage. It humiliates her by striking at the heart of her essence—her relationships. Remember, women develop self-esteem through their relationships. Having successful relationships is to a woman like accomplishing great achievements is to a man. Unfortunately women often turn this anger of betrayal against themselves, not the offending party. They internalize betrayal, believing the reason must be because they were not worthy, instead of attributing it to a man's weakness of character or another woman's vindictiveness. This self-blaming soon turns into self-loathing, which results in depression, bitterness, and anger.

But betrayal doesn't have to involve infidelity. You can betray your wife by watching porn and using it as a substitute to get your sexual needs met. Or you can betray her by throwing your life into your work. When you married her, you made a promise to "honor and cherish" her. Revolving your entire life around your job is not very honoring and it certainly doesn't make her feel cherished.

Why Meeting Her Needs Is Important

Women have different needs than men, and some of them might seem trivial to the opposite sex. For example, to my mind, my wife (and daughter) seems to be overly sensitive toward spiders, gory movies, and bathroom odors—things that don't bother me all that much, but that's just the way the women in my house roll. So I try to eliminate all those things as much as possible so they don't bother her.

One thing to keep in mind is that we are able to give to others out of our own abundance. I know, that sounds like psychobabble. But my point is that it is hard to give to others and meet their needs when we have needs ourselves—when our own emotional bank account is empty or even overdrawn. In several of my previous books for women, I often tell them that if they want their needs met, they must make sure they meet their husband's needs first (a very unpopular idea). To some degree women seem to have been created to be able to set aside their needs momentarily in order to meet the needs of others. It is probably part of their nurturing nature that they have been given this gift. They do it with their children all the time. However, even God has not given women an inexhaustible capacity of this aptitude. And the unfortunate part of this is when a woman crashes, everyone around her suffers mightily.

Therefore it behooves us as men that if we want to have our needs met, we make an effort to meet our wives' needs first. That requires us to first of all make the effort to understand what her needs are. Then we must take steps to *proactively* address them, before she even knows they are an issue—just as in the workplace, a smart manager does not wait until something breaks or a problem occurs before they address it.

In the boiler room of the Navy ship I was stationed on, we had a program called Planned Preventative Maintenance (the fact that I can even remember that after thirty years is a testament to the value of that program). This was where on a daily, weekly, and monthly basis we worked on all the pumps, boilers, evaporators, and other machinery of the fire and engine rooms. We repacked valves, replaced parts, cleaned equipment, painted deck plates, and rebuilt motors *before* they needed it. I remember as a young sailor thinking, *Why in the world are we wasting time fixing something before it breaks?* But after several years I understood the wisdom in applying preventative maintenance to items that our lives depended upon. Equipment stayed in perfect operating order so that during a crisis or an emergency we were prepared and able to deal with the problem in an efficient manner. To ignore the operating status of a pressure relief valve on a 1,200-pound boiler until it was put to the test during an emergency would put the lives of everyone on board the ship at risk. If it failed, it could explode and sink the ship, potentially killing all on board.

Our relationships are even more important. Why take the chance on having the pressure build up in your marriage until it explodes, killing the relationship and your entire family?

Intimacy-Building Tips for Fulfilling a Woman's Needs

- Tell her (and show her) that you love her and that she is beautiful every day. (This isn't rocket science, guys.) Your words are powerful and she craves compliments from you.
- Date her. Wine her and dine her. Give her an excuse to get dressed up occasionally. It makes her feel more like a woman.
- Pay attention to what makes your wife tick. What does she like? What does she dislike? What causes her to blush like a schoolgirl?

Closing

As you probably know by now, marriage is difficult, but it's hard precisely because it's so important. The marriage relationship is the bedrock of civilization. Everything in life that matters is difficult—marriage is no exception. If it didn't matter so much, it would be easy. If marriage wasn't important in God's economy, it would not be subject to so many spiritual attacks and warfare.

Not only that but developing a deeply intimate marriage relationship is even more difficult. Two separate individuals with different backgrounds, wounds, expectations, and perceptions on life come together and try to meld together as one. As different as males and females are designed physically, mentally, emotionally, and psychologically, it's a wonder we are able to relate to one another at all. And yet, there is no more powerful relationship on earth. A strongly committed husband and wife are nearly unbeatable in any situation.

Remember that truth as you go through the trials of life together. Look at your marriage with a long-range vision.

Keep the perspective that you are committed to a lifelong relationship with this person and then resolve to do all the things necessary to make that the best relationship it can possibly be. You do this with all the things that are important in your life like your career, your children, or your retirement, don't you? Why shouldn't you put that much effort in your most important relationship as well? Most importantly, remember that God has plans for your life and your marriage. Plans you don't even know about. It's really not just about you. There are people watching you and your relationship (besides your children) to see how a couple lives life together, what a good marriage looks like, and how to relate effectively to the opposite sex. Be willing to give your all to be the kind of person you yourself would love to be married to.

So we end our journey into the minds and hearts of men and women seeking to find the love, romance, and intimacy we all desire in our relationships. Hopefully you have discovered some things about your spouse, but even more importantly about yourself, that will help you nurture your marriage to become one of joy and satisfaction that lasts a lifetime. Look for the "zones" in your marriage and keep looking at the bigger picture. Appreciate the good times and learn from the struggles. Persevere through the difficulties and commit to a long-term vision of love. There is no other relationship that nurtures, grows, and completes you more than marriage. Nothing instills better health and happiness in people than a good marriage.

And always remember, your marriage matters!

Notes

Chapter 1: Marriage

1. Linda J. Waite and Maggie Gallagher, *The Case for Marriage: Why Married People Are Happier, Healthier, and Better off Financially* (New York: Broadway Books, 2002), 19.

2. Ibid., 47–67.

3. Ibid., 2–3.

4. Ibid., 192.

5. Rick I. Johnson, "Is There a Difference in Educational Outcomes in Students from Single Parent Homes?" Thesis presented to the graduate program in partial fulfillment of the requirements for the degree of Master's in Education, Concordia University Portland, 2009.

6. "No. 70: Live Births, Deaths, Marriages, and Divorces: 1950–2002," http://www.census.gov/prod/2004pubs/04statab/vitstat.pdf; M.L.Munson and P. D. Sutton, "Births, Marriages, Divorces, and Deaths: Provisional Data for 2004," Table A, "Provisional Vital Statistics for the United States," *National Vital Statistics Reports*, vol. 53, no. 21 (Hyattsville, MD: National Center for Health Statistics. 2005), updated Feb. 15, 2006, http://www.cdc.gov/nchs/data/nvsr/nvsr53/nvsr53_21.pdf; Glenn Stanton, "Divorce," Focus on the Family, http://www.focusonthefamily.com/lifechallenges/relationship_challenges/divorce.aspx?p=1.

7. Family Law: Separation, Divorce & Child Custody, "How Long Does the Average Marriage Last in the United States," January 17, 2013 (gathered from US Census Bureau data), http://familylawdivorceonline.wordpress.com/2013/01/17/how-long-does-the-average-marriage-last-in-the-united-states/.

8. "Why Married Parents Are Important for Children," For Your Marriage, http://www.foryourmarriage.org/married-parents-are-important-for-children/.

9. Kay Hymowitz, W. Bradford Wilcox, and Kelleen Kaye, "The New Unmarried Moms,"*Wall Street Journal*, March 15, 2013, http://online.wsj.com/article/SB10001424127887323826704578356494206134184.html.

10. Statistics gleaned from Johnson, "Is There a Difference in Educational Outcomes?"

11. Benjamin Scafidi, *The Taxpayer Costs of Divorce and Unwed Childbearing—First-Ever Estimates Report for the Nation and All Fifty States* (New York: Institute for American Values, 2008), 5, 17.

12. R. E. Mueller, "The Effect of Marital Dissolution on the Labour Supply of Males and Females: Evidence from Canada," *Journal of Socio-Economics*, vol. 34, no. 6 (2005): 787–809.

13. M. D.Turvey and D. H. Olsen, *Marriage and Family Wellness: Corporate America's Business?* (Minneapolis: Life Innovations, 2006).

14. Waite and Gallagher, *The Case for Marriage*, 115.

Chapter 2: Communicating with the Other Sex

1. Robert Redford and Delle Boton, *Jeremiah Johnson*, directed by Sydney Pollack (1972; Burbank, CA: Warner Home Video, 2007).

2. Gary Thomas, *Sacred Marriage* (Grand Rapids: Zondervan, 2000), 162.

3. Susie Davis, "On Marriage and Muddling Through . . . ," blog, April 3, 2013, http://www.susiedavis.org/2013/04/on-marriage-and-muddling-through/.

4. Thomas, *Sacred Marriage*, 154.

5. Gleaned from David Schnarch, *Passionate Marriage: Keeping Love & Intimacy Alive in Committed Relationships* (New York: W. W. Norton & Co., 2009), 336–38.

6. Ibid., 169.

7. Ibid., 341–42.

8. Laura Schlessinger, *The Proper Care and Feeding of Marriage* (New York: HarperCollins, 2007), 242.

9. Ibid., 170–73.

Chapter 3: Love

1. Portland Relationship Center Newsletter, August 2012, https://mail.google.com/mail/u/1/?shva=1#inbox/13926af0b3d0971e.

2. Aubrey Andelin, *Man of Steel and Velvet* (Pierce City, MO: Pacific Press Santa Barbara, 1972), 54–55.

3. Thomas, *Sacred Marriage*, 49.

4. Jancee Dunn, "Is Your Marriage Normal or Nuts?" *Reader's Digest*, May 2013, 132.

5. Jim Burns, *Creating an Intimate Marriage* (Minneapolis: Bethany, 2006), 41.

6. Eric Metaxas, "The Kids Are (Not Quite) All Right: Millennials and Narcissism," CP Opinion, May 28, 2013, http://www.christianpost.com/news/the-kids-are-not-quite-all-right-millennials-and-narcissism-96786/#yCbc0skjmzz4TZXi.99.

7. Thomas, *Sacred Marriage*, 48.

Chapter 4: Romance and Intimacy

1. Marcus Brotherton, *The Marriage Manifesto: 10 Simple Commitments Husbands Can Make That Lead to Stronger Marriages*, ebook, 2013, 17.

2. Burns, *Creating an Intimate Marriage*, 26.

3. Dennis Rainey, "5 Romantic Needs of a Woman,"FamilyLife, http://www.familylife.com/articles/topics/marriage/staying-married/romance-and-sex/5-romantic-needs-of-a-woman#.UddZGjvVB2U.

4. Schlessinger, *Proper Care & Feeding of Marriage*, 214.

5. Schnarch, *Passionate Marriage*, 199.

6. Benedict Carey, "Evidence That Little Touches Do Mean So Much," Health, *New York Times*, Feb. 22, 2010, http://www.nytimes.com/2010/02/23/health/23mind.html?_r=2&.

7. Family Resource Association, "Hand Holding Connects," August 14, 2013, http://d69fra.org/index.php?option=com_content&view=article&id=136:holding-hands-connects&catid=40:family-life-articles&Itemid=224.

8. Schnarch, *Passionate Marriage*, 102.

9. Burns, *Creating an Intimate Marriage*, 103–7.

10. Thomas, *Sacred Marriage*, 101.

Chapter 5: Sexuality

1. Schnarch, *Passionate Marriage*, 75–81.

2. Waite and Gallagher, *The Case for Marriage*, 79–91.

3. Schnarch, *Passionate Marriage*, 132–34.

4. Luke Gilkerson, "10 Surprising Porn Stats," Covenant Eyes, Breaking Free Blog, September 10, 2013, http://www.covenanteyes.com/2013/09/10/10-surprising-pornography-stats/?utm_source=twitterfeed&utm_medium=facebook.

Chapter 6: Our Woundedness

1. "Child Maltreatment 2011," US Department of Health & Human Services, Administration on Children, Youth and Families, Children's Bureau (2012), ix. Available from http://www.acf.hhs.gov/programs/cb/research-data-technology/statistics-research/child-maltreatment.

2. Schnarch, *Passionate Marriage*, 51.

3. Ibid., 56.

4. Ibid., 69.

5. Ibid., 60.

6. Ibid., 60–61.

Chapter 7: His Needs (for Her)

1. John Bene, "I'm Always Angry," Third Option Men blogspot, May 25, 2012, http://www.thirdoptionmen.org/blog/hulk-smash/.

2. Rick Johnson, *The Marriage of Your Dreams* (Grand Rapids: Revell, 2012), 148.

3. Bene, "I'm Always Angry."

4. Scott Haltzman, *The Secrets of Happily Married Women* (San Francisco: Jossey-Bass, 2008), 19–21.

5. Ibid., 19–21.

6. Shaunti Feldhahn, "Feeling Disrespected Evokes Anger in Men," blog post, 2/27/13, http://www.shaunti.com/2013/02/feeling-disrespected-evokes-anger-in -men-2/.

Chapter 8: Her Needs (for Him)

1. Patricia McGerr, "Johnny Lingo's Eight-Cow Wife," *Woman's Day*, Nov. 1965.

2. Steven Smith and David Marcum, *Catalyst: How Confidence Reacts with Our Strengths to Shape What We Achieve and Who We Become* (Highland, UT: Veracity, LC, 2014), 5.

3. Lucille Zimmerman, *Renewed* (Nashville: Abingdon Press, 2013), 4.

Rick Johnson is a bestselling author of *That's My Son*; *That's My Teenage Son*; *That's My Girl*; *Better Dads, Stronger Sons*; and *Becoming Your Spouse's Better Half*. He is the founder of Better Dads and is a sought-after speaker at many large parenting and marriage conferences across the United States and Canada. Rick, his wife, Suzanne, and their grown children live in Oregon. To find out more about Rick Johnson, visit www.betterdads.net.

Meet

RICK JOHNSON

at www.BetterDads.net

Connect with Rick on Facebook

 *Rick Johnson*

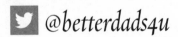 *@betterdads4u*

YOUR RECIPE FOR MARITAL SUCCESS

Learn how to use your differences to add spice and
passion to your marriage.

Revell
a division of Baker Publishing Group
www.RevellBooks.com